"Hard work plays the resonant chord,
self-reflection conducts the harmonious melody,
and sustainability orchestrates the enduring legacy"

ISBN 978-0-9763065-4-2 (paperback)

Book Cover and Inside Art by Cyphur + Art & Design

To my beloved daughters,

You are the living testament to the values and principles I
hold dear in life and leadership. Your unwavering support,
boundless love, and unbreakable spirit inspire every word
within these pages. May 'The Expansive Method' serve as
a guiding light on your own journeys, reminding you that
hard work, self-reflection, and sustainability are the building
blocks of not just leadership but a life well-lived. With all
my love and gratitude, this book is dedicated to you, my
endless source of inspiration.

With love,
Pops

THE EXPANSIVE METHOD

Building Strong Leadership Brands

JONES

Contents

FOREWARD
2

INTRODUCTION
5

Chapter 1
THE FOUNDATIONS OF LEADERSHIP
11

Chapter 2
HARD WORK AS THE CORNERSTONE
17

Chapter 3
MENTAL STRENGTH: THE POWER WITHIN
25

Chapter 4
SELF-DISCIPLINE: THE KEY TO CONSISTENCY
33

Chapter 5
SUSTAINABILITY: THE GLUE TO LEADERSHIP
41

Chapter 6
COMMUNICATION: THE LEADER'S VOICE
49

Chapter 7
EVALUATION: THE PATH TO IMPROVEMENT
57

Chapter 8
ACCOUNTABILITY: OWNING YOUR LEADERSHIP
65

Contents

Chapter 9
THE TEM™ APPROACH IN ACTION
73

Chapter 10
TEM™ IN SELF LEADERSHIP CONTEXT
83

Chapter 11
TEM™ IN ONE TO ONE LEADERSHIP CONTEXT
93

Chapter 12
TEM™ IN TEAM LEADERSHIP CONTEXT
101

Chapter 13
TEM™ IN ORGANIZATIONAL LEADERSHIP CONTEXT
109

Chapter 14
TEM™ IN ALLIANCE LEADERSHIP CONTEXT
117

ANALYSIS
THE EXPANSIVE METHOD:
A BLUEPRINT FOR EXCEPTIONAL LEADERSHIP
125

APPENDIX A
131

APPENDIX B
171

BIBLIOGRAPHY
174

INDEX
177

THE
EXPANSIVE
METHOD

Building Strong Leadership Brands

JONES

Foreward

It is a rare privilege to come across a guide that stands apart from the rest, an offering that doesn't dwell in the realm of platitudes and abstractions but delves deep into the trenches of experience. The tome you hold in your hands is precisely that—a no-nonsense blueprint for constructing robust Leadership Brands.

Our dad, the author of this masterpiece, without explicitly naming himself, has embarked on a remarkable journey across multiple industries, leaving an indelible mark on each. From the corporate boardrooms to the arenas of sports, from the battlefields of philanthropy to the classrooms of mentorship, our dad's footprint can be traced through a myriad of transformative experiences.

For those who may wonder about the authenticity of this guide, rest assured that it is not born of mere theorizing or armchair philosophy. Instead, it is the outcome of years spent in the crucible of real-world leadership, where victories and setbacks become the crucible of wisdom.

Our dad's style, reminiscent of the fearless and unapologetic Frederick Douglass, weaves a narrative that is unafraid to cut through the noise. Like a seasoned intellectual dissecting game-winning strategies, this guide dissects the intricacies of leadership with a sharp and discerning eye. It doesn't shy away from the tough questions or gloss over the complexities; instead, it confronts them head-on, just as Douglass unapologetically tackled the issues of his day.

"The Expansive Method," the framework at the core of this guide, isn't a mere academic construct. It's a battle-tested arsenal of principles that have been tried, refined, and honed through the fires of leadership challenges. Much like Douglass' unwavering commitment to spreadingthe truth, our dad's devotion to dissecting leadership and distilling its essence is evident in every chapter.

This guide transcends the mundane and provides a comprehensive toolkit for building Leadership Brands that endure. It's a testament to his passion for excellence and a reflection of a career devoted to pushing the boundaries of what leadership can achieve.

As you read the pages of this remarkable work, channel your inner Douglass, and embrace the unvarnished truth about leadership. Absorb the wisdom distilled from years of diverse experiences across industries and disciplines. Let this guide be your compass as you embark on your own leadership journey, guided by the principles of The Expansive Method, and may it illuminate your path towards building a Leadership Brand that stands the test of time.

4 |

Introduction

The Beginning

Leadership stands as a critical pillar supporting the success and longevity of organizations, whether they are businesses, nonprofits, educational institutions, or government entities. Leadership, in this contemporary context, is not merely about occupying a position of authority, but rather, it embodies a dynamic and multifaceted concept that drives and inspires individuals and groups toward shared objectives and visions. Effective leadership transcends titles and formal hierarchies; it is the driving force behind innovation, growth, and the attainment of goals. It is the essence of what we call a leadership brand.

In this book, we delve into the art and science of building strong leadership brands through a systematic and actionable approach known as The Expansive Methodology, or TEM™ for short. TEM™ represents a comprehensive framework that emphasizes the cultivation of four fundamental character traits and personal philosophies that are intrinsically connected to driving positive productivity in leadership.

Before we embark on this journey through TEM™, let us first grasp the significance of leadership brands and why they matter more than ever in today's fast-paced and interconnected world.

The Significance of Leadership Brands

Imagine leadership as the compass guiding an organization through uncharted waters, and leadership brand as the unique map that charts the course and distinguishes one voyage from another. Leadership brands encapsulate the essence of a leader's identity, values, and impact. They represent a leader's ability to influence, inspire, and make a lasting impression on those they lead.

In the contemporary landscape, where competition is fierce and change is constant, leadership brands have become indispensable. They provide a sense of direction and authenticity that enables organizations to attract top talent, foster innovation, and retain loyal stakeholders. Leadership brands serve as a lodestar for employees seeking purpose in their work, investors seeking long-term value, and customers seeking products or services aligned with their values.

Consider some of the world's most renowned leaders, and you'll notice that their names evoke specific qualities and associations. For instance, when you think of Nelson Mandela, you may associate his leadership brand with resilience, forgiveness, and social justice. When you think of Steve Jobs, innovation, design, and disruptive thinking may come to mind. These leaders didn't merely occupy positions of authority; they crafted their leadership brands deliberately over time, which, in turn, solidified their enduring legacies.

The TEM™ Approach

Now, let us turn our attention to The Expansive Methodology, TEM™, a strategic framework designed to help individuals and organizations build robust leadership brands. At its core, TEM™ is founded on a bottom-up approach, emphasizing the cultivation of four key character traits and personal philosophies that are inexorably tied to enhanced productivity in leadership roles.

1. Hard Work

The first pillar of TEM™, hard work, is a testament to the timeless principle that success is often a direct result of effort, dedication, and unrelenting perseverance. It transcends talent, relying instead on the willingness to invest time, energy, and sweat equity in the relentless pursuit of improvement. Leaders who embody this trait commit themselves wholeheartedly to the continuous striving for excellence, recognizing that the journey itself holds immense value.

Hard work is not confined to the realm of innate abilities or natural talents; it is accessible to all who are willing to exert maximum effort. Whether you're an aspiring leader or a seasoned one, the capacity to invest your time and energy in the relentless pursuit of personal and organizational growth is an essential component of your leadership brand.

2. Mental Strength

The second pillar, mental strength, underscores the paramount importance of psychological resilience and fortitude in the realm of leadership. It poses the question: Are you mentally equipped to navigate the tumultuous seas of challenges, setbacks, and demanding work environments? True leaders demonstrate an acute mentality that empowers them to persevere when confronted with adversity and uncertainty.

Incorporating mental strength into your leadership brand means possessing the unwavering determination to push through even when faced with the most daunting obstacles. It involves the ability to maintain composure, focus, and resolve in the face of adversity, inspiring those around you to follow suit.

3. Self-Discipline

The third pillar, self-discipline, represents the linchpin that holds together the structural integrity of leadership brands. It encapsulates the capacity to consistently do what is right, at the right time and place, even in the absence of external oversight. Leaders who embody self-discipline maintain a steadfast commitment to their responsibilities, obligations, and ethical principles.

To integrate self-discipline into your leadership brand means adhering to a personal code of conduct that emphasizes doing your job with unwavering consistency and integrity. It involves the ability to assess one's performance objectively, acknowledge areas of improvement, and have the discipline to take deliberate actions to enhance one's effectiveness.

4. Sustainability

The fourth and final pillar, sustainability, represents the culmination of the previous three traits. Sustainability is not a standalone concept but rather the product of hard work, mental strength, and self-discipline working harmoniously over time. It reflects the ability to perpetuate these actions consistently, ensuring that they become enduring components of one's leadership brand.

Without sustainability, leadership is akin to a flickering flame that burns brightly for a moment but ultimately fizzles out. Leaders who prioritize sustainability recognize that it is not enough to work hard sporadically, display mental strength in fleeting moments, or exercise self-discipline occasionally. True leadership necessitates the capacity to sustain these actions consistently over the long haul.

Communication, Evaluation, and Accountability

While the four pillars of TEM™ form the core of building a leadership brand, they are not isolated principles. In fact, they are intricately connected to three essential elements of leadership: communication, evaluation, and accountability.

Effective communication serves as the conduit through which leaders convey their vision, values, and expectations to their teams. It is the means by which leaders inspire, inform, and engage those they lead. Through effective communication, leaders foster understanding, alignment, and a sense of purpose among their followers.

Evaluation, on the other hand, is the compass by which leaders navigate their journey toward improvement. It involves the continuous assessment of one's performance, decisions, and outcomes. Leaders who embrace evaluation view it not as a judgment but as a catalyst for growth. They recognize that self-awareness and a commitment to self-improvement are essential components of sustained success.

Accountability, the third element, underlines the importance of ownership in leadership. Leaders who hold themselves accountable for their actions, decisions, and outcomes demonstrate integrity and authenticity. Accountability is the cornerstone of trust-building, both within and outside the organization. Leaders who take responsibility for their actions inspire confidence and foster an environment of transparency and ethical conduct.

In the pages that follow...

...we will explore each of these principles in depth, providing practical insights, real-world examples, and actionable strategies to help you build and strengthen your leadership brand. The Expansive Methodology, TEM™, is not a mere theoretical construct; it is a dynamic and pragmatic approach that can be applied by leaders at all levels, in diverse fields, and across various contexts.

As we journey together through the chapters ahead, you will gain a profound understanding of how hard work, mental strength, self-discipline, and sustainability form the bedrock of your leadership brand. You will discover how communication, evaluation, and accountability serve as the pillars that elevate your brand to new heights of influence and impact.

Our objective is clear: to empower you to become a leader who not only navigates the complexities of the modern world but also leaves an indelible mark, a leader whose brand resonates with authenticity, purpose, and enduring value. The Expansive Methodology is your guide on this transformative journey—a journey toward building a strong and enduring leadership brand that stands as a testament to your vision, your values, and your unwavering commitment to excellence.

Now, let us begin the exploration of TEM™ and the principles that will shape your leadership journey for years to come.

Chapter 1

The Foundations of Leadership

Leadership in the Modern World

Leadership is not merely about occupying positions of authority. It transcends titles and formal hierarchies, embodying a dynamic and multifaceted concept that drives and inspires individuals and groups toward shared objectives and visions. Effective leadership has become the linchpin supporting the success and longevity of organizations, whether they are businesses, nonprofits, educational institutions, or government entities.

At its essence, leadership involves the ability to influence, motivate, and make a lasting impression on those you lead. It's about charting a course, setting a direction, and navigating through uncharted waters. Leadership, in this context, is not a solitary endeavor but a collaborative one, where leaders work in tandem with their teams to achieve common goals. It's about fostering innovation, growth, and the attainment of objectives. It's about being the compass that guides the organization through the complexities and uncertainties of the modern world.

Leadership Brand: Beyond Titles

When we speak of leadership in the modern context, we introduce the concept of a leadership brand. A leadership brand represents the unique identity, values, and impact of a leader. It encapsulates what a leader stands for, how they inspire, and the legacy they leave behind. A leadership brand is the essence of leadership in action.

Think of a leadership brand as the map that charts the course of a leader's journey. It distinguishes one leader from another and evokes specific qualities and associations. It's not merely a label or a title; it's a powerful narrative that communicates a leader's identity and influence.

Leadership brands matter more than ever in today's fast-paced and interconnected world. They provide a sense of direction and authenticity that enables organizations to attract top talent, foster innovation, and retain loyal stakeholders. Leadership brands serve as a lodestar for employees seeking purpose in their work, investors seeking long-term value, and customers seeking products or services aligned with their values.

The Evolution of Leadership

The concept of leadership has evolved over the years. It has shifted from the traditional top-down, command-and-control model to a more inclusive, collaborative, and adaptive approach. In today's organizations, leadership is not confined to a select few at the top; it can emerge from any level, and it is valued for its ability to inspire and drive results.

Leadership today is characterized by:

Adaptability: Effective leaders must navigate rapidly changing environments and respond to evolving challenges. They must be flexible, open to new ideas, and willing to pivot when necessary.

Empowerment: Leaders empower their teams, granting them the autonomy and authority to make decisions and take ownership of their work. Empowerment fosters a sense of ownership and accountability.

Inclusivity: Inclusive leadership recognizes the value of diverse perspectives and experiences. It seeks to create an environment where all voices are heard and all talents are leveraged.

Emotional Intelligence: Leaders with emotional intelligence understand and manage their own emotions and those of others. They are empathetic, able to build strong relationships, and skilled in resolving conflicts.

Purpose-Driven: Leaders today are expected to lead with purpose, aligning their actions with a meaningful vision that inspires others. Purpose-driven leaders are guided by a sense of mission and a commitment to making a positive impact.

Continuous Learning: In a world of constant change, leaders must be continuous learners. They seek opportunities to develop their skills, expand their knowledge, and stay relevant in their fields.

Building Blocks of Leadership

To understand leadership and its foundations, we must break it down into its constituent elements. These elements serve as the building blocks upon which effective leadership is constructed. They are the essential components that make up the leadership brand.

Character: At the heart of leadership lies character. Character encompasses the qualities and values that define a leader. It involves integrity, honesty, ethics, and a commitment to doing what is right. Character forms the bedrock of trust, which is essential for effective leadership. A leader's character is not solely about what they say; it's about how they behave and the example they set.

Vision: Leadership is about charting a course toward a vision. A leader's vision is a clear and compelling picture of a better future. It serves as a guidepost, directing actions and inspiring others to follow. A well-articulated vision provides focus and purpose, aligning the efforts of a team or organization.

Communication: Effective communication is the bridge between a leader's vision and its realization. Leaders must be adept at conveying their ideas, values, and expectations. Communication involves not only speaking but also listening actively and empathetically. It's about fostering understanding, building relationships, and inspiring action.

Influence: Leadership is fundamentally about influence. Leaders persuade, motivate, and guide others toward shared goals. Influence is not about coercion or manipulation but about inspiring voluntary cooperation. It's about convincing others that the path forward is worth following.

Resilience: In the face of adversity and setbacks, leaders must demonstrate resilience. Resilience involves the ability to bounce back from challenges, adapt to change, and persevere in the pursuit of objectives. Resilient leaders inspire confidence and provide stability in turbulent times.

Adaptability: In a rapidly changing world, leaders must be adaptable. They must embrace change, learn from failure, and adjust their strategies as needed. Adaptability is the capacity to pivot when circumstances demand it, without losing sight of the overarching vision.

Empathy: Leaders who demonstrate empathy connect with others on a deeper level. They understand the perspectives and emotions of those they lead. Empathy fosters trust, collaboration, and a sense of belonging within a team or organization.

Accountability: Accountability is the cornerstone of responsible leadership. Leaders hold themselves and others accountable for their actions, decisions, and outcomes. Accountability is not about blame but about taking ownership and learning from mistakes.

In the chapters that follow, we will delve into each of these building blocks of leadership in greater detail. We will explore how they intersect, how they can be cultivated and strengthened, and how they contribute to the formation of a robust leadership brand.

The Expansive Methodology (TEM™)

To build a strong leadership brand, we need a structured and actionable approach. That's where The Expansive Methodology, or TEM™, comes into play. TEM™ represents a comprehensive framework that emphasizes the cultivation of four fundamental character traits and personal philosophies. These traits are intrinsically connected to driving positive productivity in leadership roles.

In the chapters ahead, we will explore these four pillars of TEM™ in depth:

Hard Work: The willingness to invest time, effort, and sweat equity in the relentless pursuit of improvement.

Mental Strength: The ability to persevere and maintain composure in the face of adversity and uncertainty.

Self-Discipline: The commitment to consistently do what is right, at the right time and place, with unwavering integrity.

Sustainability: The capacity to perpetuate hard work, mental strength, and self-discipline consistently over the long term.

Each of these pillars is not only a standalone principle but also an integral component of the leadership building blocks we discussed earlier. They are the bedrock upon which leadership brands are built, and they are accessible to leaders at all levels and in various contexts.

As we embark on this journey through TEM™, we will provide practical insights, real-world examples, and actionable strategies to help you cultivate these traits and incorporate them into your leadership brand. Our goal is to empower you to become a leader who not only navigates the complexities of the modern world but also leaves an indelible mark—a leader whose brand resonates with authenticity, purpose, and enduring value.

Now, let's begin our exploration of the first pillar of TEM™: hard work—the foundation upon which strong leadership brands are built.

Chapter 2

Hard Work
as the Cornerstone

Hard work stands as the cornerstone upon which strong leadership brands are built. It is an unwavering commitment to investing time, effort, and sweat equity in the relentless pursuit of improvement. Hard work transcends talent and innate abilities; it is the universal currency of achievement, accessible to all who are willing to exert maximum effort.

The Nature of Hard Work

Hard work, at its essence, is about determination, perseverance, and the unyielding pursuit of excellence. It is the recognition that success is not bestowed upon a select few based on inherent advantages, but rather, it is a product of sustained effort and dedication. Whether you're an aspiring leader or a seasoned one, the capacity to work diligently and tenaciously is a fundamental building block of your leadership brand.

Hard work is not a one-time endeavor; it's a way of life. It entails the daily commitment to pushing your limits, expanding your capabilities, and relentlessly pursuing improvement. It is the embodiment of the principle that success is not a destination but a journey—a journey marked by continuous growth and evolution.

The Work Ethic Paradox

In today's world, there is a paradox surrounding the concept of hard work. On one hand, we live in an era characterized by convenience and instant gratification. Technological advancements have streamlined many aspects of our lives, offering the allure of ease and efficiency. On the other hand, the pursuit of excellence, the cultivation of expertise, and the attainment of significant goals still demand one thing above all else: hard work.

The paradox lies in the fact that while technology has made certain tasks easier and more accessible, it has not diminished the necessity of hard work in achieving meaningful accomplishments. In fact, in many cases, it has raised the bar for what constitutes excellence. The digital age demands adaptability, continuous learning, and a relentless work ethic.

The Myth of Overnight Success

In a world of instant updates and viral sensations, it's easy to fall into the trap of believing in overnight success stories. We see individuals and organizations seemingly rise to prominence with lightning speed, and we are tempted to believe that success can be achieved effortlessly. However, such stories often conceal the countless hours of hard work, dedication, and perseverance that preceded the breakthrough moment.

The reality is that genuine success, especially in leadership, is rarely a sudden phenomenon. It is the culmination of consistent effort and a commitment to improvement over an extended period. Leaders who appear to achieve success rapidly have often honed their skills, endured setbacks, and invested significant time and energy behind the scenes.

The Growth Mindset

One of the key principles that underpin the value of hard work is the growth mindset. Coined by psychologist Carol Dweck, the growth mindset is the belief that abilities and intelligence can be developed through dedication and hard work. In contrast, a fixed mindset assumes that abilities are innate and unchangeable.

Leaders with a growth mindset see challenges as opportunities for learning and growth. They embrace setbacks as stepping stones toward improvement. Instead of shying away from difficulties, they tackle them head-on, knowing that hard work and effort will ultimately lead to mastery.

Cultivating a growth mindset involves:

Embracing Challenges: Rather than avoiding challenges, seek them out as opportunities to expand your skills and knowledge.

Persisting in the Face of Setbacks: When you encounter obstacles or failures, view them as temporary setbacks and persist in your efforts to overcome them.

Seeing Effort as a Path to Mastery: Understand that hard work and effort are prerequisites for mastery in any field.

Learning from Criticism: Welcome constructive criticism as a means to improve, rather than as a personal attack.

Finding Inspiration in Others' Success: Instead of feeling threatened by the success of others, find inspiration in their achievements and use them as benchmarks for your own growth.

The Role of Discipline

Hard work and discipline go hand in hand. Discipline is the ability to structure your actions and behaviors in alignment with your goals and values. It is the commitment to doing what needs to be done, even when you may not feel like doing it. Discipline ensures that hard work becomes a consistent and sustainable practice.

To cultivate discipline in your leadership journey:

Set Clear Goals: Define your objectives and break them down into manageable tasks.

Establish Routines: Create daily and weekly routines that prioritize tasks that align with your goals.

Eliminate Distractions: Identify and eliminate distractions that can derail your focus and productivity.

Hold Yourself Accountable: Take responsibility for your actions and hold yourself to a high standard of performance.

Seek Support: Surround yourself with individuals who support your goals and can help you stay accountable.

The Perseverance Mindset

Perseverance is the unwavering commitment to a course of action, even in the face of difficulties and adversity. It is an essential attribute of leaders who excel in the long run. Perseverance recognizes that challenges and setbacks are not roadblocks but detours on the path to success.

To embrace a perseverance mindset:

Maintain Resilience: Develop the ability to bounce back from setbacks and adapt to changing circumstances.

Focus on Long-Term Goals: Keep your eye on the big picture and don't be discouraged by short-term setbacks.

Learn from Failures: View failures as opportunities for learning and growth.

Seek Support: Lean on your support network for encouragement and guidance during challenging times.

Stay Committed: Commit to your goals and stay dedicated to your vision, even when faced with obstacles.

Leaders Who Embody Hard Work

Throughout history, leaders who have left a lasting impact are those who embodied the principles of hard work, discipline, and perseverance. Their stories serve as inspiration and proof that the path to leadership excellence is paved with effort and dedication.

Bryan Stevenson: Bryan Stevenson, a lawyer and founder of the Equal Justice Initiative, has tirelessly advocated for criminal justice reform and the rights of the marginalized. His dedication to the cause of justice and equality is unwavering.

Barack Obama: The 44th President of the United States, Barack Obama, is known for his dedication to public service and tireless work ethic. His journey from community organizing to the presidency reflects his commitment to making a positive impact on society.

Oprah Winfrey: Media mogul Oprah Winfrey's journey from a troubled childhood to global success is a story of perseverance and hard work. She overcame numerous obstacles to build her media empire and become a symbol of empowerment.

Shonda Rhimes: The renowned television producer and writer, Shonda Rhimes, has achieved immense success through her dedication to storytelling. Her work on hit shows like "Grey's Anatomy" and "Scandal" is a testament to her creative and professional commitment.

Malala Yousafzai: Nobel laureate Malala Yousafzai's advocacy for girls' education in the face of adversity showcases the impact of perseverance. Despite facing life-threatening challenges, she continues to work tirelessly to ensure every girl's right to an education.

These leaders, among many others, exemplify the transformative potential of hard work and dedication. Their stories remind us that the path to leadership excellence demands unwavering commitment and effort.

Practical Steps to Embrace Hard Work

Embracing hard work as the cornerstone of your leadership journey within the TEM™ framework is a transformative decision, one that requires deliberate actions and a commitment to continuous improvement. Here are practical steps to wholeheartedly embrace the essence of hard work and integrate it into your leadership brand:

Set Clear Goals and Priorities:
Begin by setting clear, well-defined goals for yourself and your team. Prioritize these objectives based on their significance and alignment with your organization's vision. Clarity in goals helps channel your hard work effectively.

Create a Personal Work Ethic Code:
Develop a personal code of work ethic that encapsulates your commitment to hard work. This code can serve as a guiding light during challenging times, reminding you of your unwavering dedication.

Time Management and Productivity Tools:
Implement time management and productivity tools to optimize your workflow. These tools can help you allocate your time efficiently, ensuring that your hard work yields the maximum output.

Celebrate Small Wins:
Acknowledge and celebrate small victories and achievements along the way. Recognizing progress, no matter how minor, fuels motivation and reinforces the value of hard work.

Encourage Open Communication:
Foster an environment of open communication within your team. Encourage team members to share their ideas, concerns, and feedback. Communication is vital for aligning everyone's efforts with the overarching goals that hard work seeks to achieve.

Mentorship and Coaching:
Seek mentorship and coaching from experienced leaders who embody the principles of hard work. Learning from their journeys can provide valuable insights and guidance as you navigate your own path.

Adaptability and Resilience:
Develop adaptability and resilience as essential companions to hard work. Understand that setbacks and challenges are an inherent part of leadership. Your ability to bounce back and adapt to changing circumstances complements your dedication.

Continuous Learning:
Embrace a mindset of continuous learning. Stay curious and open to acquiring new knowledge and skills. A commitment to personal growth is a testament to your dedication to improvement through hard work.

Delegate Effectively:
Recognize that hard work doesn't mean doing everything yourself. Effective delegation ensures that tasks are distributed according to strengths and expertise, maximizing overall productivity.

Lead by Empowerment:
Empower your team members to take ownership of their roles and responsibilities. When individuals feel empowered, they are more likely to invest their own hard work and dedication into their work.

Evaluate and Adjust:
Regularly evaluate your progress and the outcomes of your hard work. Be willing to adjust your strategies and approaches based on what you learn from both successes and setbacks.

Reinforce Ethical Conduct:
Uphold ethical conduct as a non-negotiable aspect of hard work. Ensure that your dedication to success is firmly rooted in ethical principles and responsible practices.

Inspire Others:
Finally, inspire those around you with your unwavering commitment to hard work. Be the beacon of diligence that encourages others to embrace the path of continuous improvement and relentless effort.

In your leadership journey, embracing hard work as the cornerstone is not a static destination but a dynamic process of growth and refinement. It's a commitment to both personal and collective betterment, and it's the unwavering dedication to realizing not just short-term victories but long-lasting success. Remember that hard work, within the TEM™ framework, is not merely about exertion; it's about the energy, passion, and relentless pursuit of excellence that you bring to every endeavor. It is, without a doubt, the enduring cornerstone upon which you can construct a leadership brand that stands the test of time, inspires others, and leaves an indelible mark on the world of leadership.

Chapter 3

Mental Strength:
The Power Within

Mental strength emerges as a formidable thread—one that weaves resilience, fortitude, and unwavering determination into the very fabric of effective leadership. It is the power within, the indomitable spirit that enables leaders to navigate tumultuous waters, overcome adversity, and persevere in the face of formidable challenges. Mental strength is not an abstract concept; it is a tangible asset, a quality that separates extraordinary leaders from the ordinary.

Understanding Mental Strength

Mental strength, in its essence, is the capacity to harness the power of one's mind to confront and conquer obstacles, setbacks, and demanding circumstances. It goes beyond raw intelligence or knowledge; it encompasses the ability to maintain composure, focus, and resolve in times of difficulty. Leaders who embody mental strength exhibit qualities such as resilience, determination, and the fortitude to power through even when the path ahead is steep and treacherous.

The Acute Mentality

At the core of mental strength lies what can be described as the "acute mentality." It's the mindset that drives leaders to persevere relentlessly when situations, environments, or work becomes difficult and demanding. This acute mentality is not a rare trait reserved for a select few; rather, it is a quality that can be cultivated and nurtured by anyone aspiring to become an effective leader.

Leaders with an acute mentality demonstrate the following characteristics:

Resilience: They bounce back from setbacks, learning from failures, and emerging stronger.

Determination: They exhibit unwavering resolve and stay committed to their goals, even in the face of adversity.

Adaptability: They embrace change and remain flexible in response to shifting circumstances.

Mental Endurance: They have the stamina to tackle challenging tasks and maintain focus over extended periods.

Optimism: They maintain a positive outlook, even when confronted with challenging situations.

The Power of Resilience

Resilience, a cornerstone of mental strength, is the capacity to recover quickly from difficulties or setbacks. It's the ability to bounce back when faced with adversity and emerge stronger than before. Resilient leaders view challenges as opportunities for growth and learning rather than insurmountable obstacles.

Building resilience involves:

Developing a Growth Mindset: Embrace challenges as opportunities for personal and professional development.

Maintaining Perspective: Keep challenges in perspective and avoid magnifying their significance.

Practicing Self-Care: Prioritize physical and emotional well-being through healthy habits, stress management, and self-compassion.

Building a Support Network: Lean on friends, family, mentors, and colleagues for support during challenging times.

Learning from Setbacks: Analyze failures and setbacks to extract valuable lessons and adjust strategies accordingly.

Determination: The Unyielding Resolve

Determination is the unwavering resolve to achieve goals and persist in the pursuit of one's vision. It's the commitment to keep moving forward, even when faced with obstacles that seem insurmountable. Determined leaders possess an inner fire—a burning desire to achieve, excel, and make a difference.

To cultivate determination:

Set Clear Goals: Define your objectives with clarity and specificity.

Break Goals into Actionable Steps: Divide large goals into smaller, manageable tasks to maintain a sense of progress.

Stay Focused: Concentrate your efforts on high-priority tasks that align with your goals.

Visualize Success: Envision your goals as already achieved, which can fuel your determination.

Stay Accountable: Share your goals with others who can provide support and hold you accountable.

Adaptability in Leadership

The modern landscape of leadership is marked by constant change and evolving challenges. Leaders who embrace adaptability—a core aspect of mental strength—are better equipped to navigate these shifting tides. Adaptability is the capacity to adjust one's strategies, perspectives, and approaches in response to changing circumstances.

To foster adaptability:

Cultivate a Growth Mindset: Embrace change as an opportunity for learning and growth.

Stay Informed: Keep abreast of industry trends and emerging developments.

Seek Feedback: Solicit feedback from others to gain new perspectives and insights.

Remain Flexible: Be open to modifying strategies and plans as circumstances evolve.

Learn from Mistakes: View failures and setbacks as valuable lessons that inform future decisions.

Mental Endurance: The Stamina to Succeed

Leadership often demands prolonged periods of focus, effort, and concentration. Mental endurance is the capacity to maintain mental stamina and focus over extended periods. Leaders who possess mental endurance can tackle complex tasks, make critical decisions, and sustain their efforts when the going gets tough.

To enhance mental endurance:

Practice Mindfulness: Engage in mindfulness techniques to improve concentration and reduce mental fatigue.

Prioritize Sleep: Ensure you get adequate rest to maintain cognitive function and decision-making abilities.

Take Breaks: Incorporate regular breaks into your workday to recharge and maintain productivity.

Manage Stress: Implement stress management strategies, such as deep breathing or meditation, to reduce mental strain.

Stay Organized: Maintain a structured approach to tasks and responsibilities to minimize mental clutter.

Optimism: The Positive Perspective

Optimism is the unwavering belief in a favorable outcome, even in the face of adversity. Optimistic leaders approach challenges with a positive mindset, seeing opportunities where others may see obstacles. This positive perspective is contagious and can inspire teams to persevere in challenging times.

To foster optimism:

Practice Positive Self-Talk: Replace negative self-talk with constructive and optimistic language.

Focus on Solutions: Encourage a problem-solving approach rather than dwelling on problems.

Celebrate Small Wins: Acknowledge and celebrate progress, no matter how incremental.

Surround Yourself with Positivity: Spend time with individuals who uplift and inspire.

Maintain Perspective: Keep challenges in context and remind yourself of past successes.

Leaders Who Embody Mental Strength

Leaders who embody mental strength leave an indelible mark on their organizations and the people they lead. They are the bedrock of stability during times of turbulence, the guiding light in moments of darkness, and the unwavering source of inspiration. Their stories serve as a testament to the power of mental strength.

Abraham Lincoln: The 16th President of the United States faced unprecedented challenges during the Civil War. His unwavering resolve to preserve the Union and his ability to maintain composure amid immense adversity is a testament to mental strength.

Malcolm X: A civil rights activist and a powerful advocate for Black Americans, Malcolm X overcame personal hardships, including incarceration, to emerge as a influential leader. His unyielding determination to fight for justice and equality exemplified mental strength.

Angela Merkel: As the Chancellor of Germany, Angela Merkel navigated the European financial crisis and the refugee crisis with a steady hand. Her resilience and ability to maintain a cool head during tumultuous times earned her respect as a global leader.

Nelson Mandela: Imprisoned for 27 years for his anti-apartheid activism, Nelson Mandela emerged from captivity with an unbroken spirit. His ability to forgive, his unwavering commitment to reconciliation, and his determination to end apartheid showcased mental strength of the highest order.

Sheryl Sandberg: Facebook COO Sheryl Sandberg endured personal tragedy with the loss of her husband. Her resilience in the face of grief and her advocacy for resilience and leadership, as seen in her book "Option B," highlight the power of mental strength.

These leaders, among many others, demonstrate that mental strength is not an abstract concept but a concrete asset that can be developed and honed. Their stories serve as a source of inspiration for leaders seeking to cultivate their own mental strength.

Practical Steps to Strengthen Mental Strength

Cultivating mental strength is an ongoing process that involves self-awareness and deliberate practice. Here are practical steps to enhance your mental strength:

Set Realistic Expectations: Avoid setting unrealistic or unattainable goals that can lead to frustration.

Develop a Resilience Toolkit: Identify coping mechanisms and strategies that help you bounce back from setbacks.

Practice Mindfulness: Engage in mindfulness exercises to improve focus, reduce stress, and enhance mental clarity.

Seek Support: Build a support network of friends, mentors, and colleagues who can provide guidance and encouragement.

Challenge Negative Thinking: Recognize and challenge negative thought patterns that undermine your mental strength.

Embrace Change: View change as an opportunity for growth and learning rather than a threat.

Celebrate Progress: Acknowledge and celebrate your achievements and milestones, no matter how small they may seem.

Stay Physically Active: Regular physical activity can boost mental resilience and reduce stress.

Learn from Adversity: Reflect on past challenges and setbacks to extract valuable lessons for future growth.

Cultivate Optimism: Practice seeing challenges as opportunities and maintain a positive outlook.

The Transformative Power of Mental Strength

Mental strength emerges as a force that can propel leaders to new heights. It is the power within that transforms obstacles into stepping stones, setbacks into opportunities, and challenges into catalysts for growth. As you embark on your leadership journey, remember that mental strength is not a fixed attribute but a dynamic quality that can be nurtured and cultivated over time. It is the unwavering resolve that propels leaders forward, even in the face of adversity. It is the power within that defines extraordinary leadership.

Chapter 4

Self-Discipline:
The Key to Consistency

In leadership, where the path to success is often marked by unpredictable challenges and complex decisions, self-discipline emerges as the key to achieving consistency, maintaining integrity, and fortifying one's leadership brand. It is the unwavering commitment to doing what is right, at the right time and place, with unyielding integrity. Self-discipline is the compass that keeps leaders on course, ensuring that they fulfill their responsibilities and obligations with diligence and determination.

The Essence of Self-Discipline

At its core, self-discipline is the ability to control one's impulses, emotions, and behaviors in pursuit of a defined goal or set of principles. It is a conscious choice to adhere to a chosen course of action, even when faced with distractions, temptations, or adversity. Self-discipline empowers leaders to prioritize their long-term objectives over short-term gratification, making it a cornerstone of consistency and ethical leadership.

The Power of Consistency

Consistency is the hallmark of effective leadership. It is the reliability and predictability with which a leader operates, adhering to a set of values, standards, and principles. Consistent leaders inspire trust and confidence because their actions align with their words. They create a stable and cohesive environment in which their teams can thrive.

Consistency involves:

Alignment with Values: Ensuring that your actions and decisions align with your core values and principles.

Reliability: Being dependable and fulfilling your commitments consistently.

Transparency: Communicating openly and honestly, even when the message is challenging.

Predictability: Providing a sense of stability and coherence in your leadership style.

Fairness: Treating all individuals fairly and impartially.

The Discipline of Integrity

Integrity is the bedrock upon which self-discipline is built. It is the quality of being honest and having strong moral principles, even when no one is watching. Leaders with integrity are unwavering in their commitment to doing what is right, regardless of external pressures or temptations.

Integrity in leadership involves:

Ethical Decision-Making: Making choices that uphold ethical standards and principles.

Accountability: Taking responsibility for your actions and decisions, whether they lead to success or failure.

Honesty: Communicating truthfully and transparently with others.

Consistency in Values: Ensuring that your actions consistently reflect your core values.

Courage: Having the bravery to stand up for what is right, even when it is challenging.

The Discipline of Time Management

Time management is a critical component of self-discipline in leadership. Leaders who effectively manage their time can allocate their resources, including their attention, focus, and energy, to the most important tasks and responsibilities. Time management enables leaders to maintain their productivity, meet deadlines, and allocate adequate time for reflection and strategic thinking.

Effective time management involves:

Setting Priorities: Identifying the most important tasks and focusing on them first.

Creating Schedules: Developing daily, weekly, and long-term schedules to allocate time effectively.

Minimizing Distractions: Identifying and eliminating sources of distraction to maintain focus.

Delegating Responsibilities: Allocating tasks to others when appropriate to free up your time for higher-priority activities.

Strategic Planning: Setting clear goals and developing strategies to achieve them within specified timeframes.

The Discipline of Decision-Making

Effective leadership often entails making complex decisions under pressure. Self-discipline in decision-making involves maintaining a rational and objective approach, even when emotions or external factors may cloud judgment. It requires leaders to consider multiple perspectives, gather relevant information, and adhere to their principles when making choices.

Self-discipline in decision-making involves:

Emotional Regulation: Managing and controlling emotions to make rational decisions.

Active Listening: Actively seeking input and feedback from others before making decisions.

Considering Consequences: Evaluating the potential outcomes and consequences of decisions.

Ethical Considerations: Ensuring that decisions align with ethical principles and values.

Accountability: Taking ownership of the decisions made and their impacts.

The Discipline
of Feedback and Improvement

Self-discipline extends to the willingness to seek feedback and continuously improve. Leaders who possess this discipline are open to constructive criticism and self-evaluation. They recognize that self-awareness and the ability to adapt and grow are essential components of effective leadership.

The discipline of feedback and improvement involves:

Receptivity to Feedback: Welcoming feedback from colleagues, mentors, and team members.

Self-Reflection: Taking time to reflect on your actions, decisions, and outcomes.

Learning from Mistakes: Viewing failures as opportunities for learning and growth.

Goal Setting: Establishing personal and professional development goals.

Adaptability: Adjusting your approach and behaviors based on feedback and self-assessment.

Leaders Who Embody Self-Discipline

Leaders who embody self-discipline are the compasses that guide their organizations toward ethical and consistent performance. Their actions are consistent with their values, and their decisions are made with integrity and accountability. They inspire trust, confidence, and respect, serving as role models for others to emulate.

Warren Buffett: The billionaire investor is renowned for his disciplined approach to investing and his adherence to a set of core values and principles. His consistency in decision-making and long-term perspective have earned him a reputation as one of the most successful investors of all time.

Indra Nooyi: The former CEO of PepsiCo demonstrated self-discipline by consistently prioritizing health and sustainability initiatives during her tenure. She navigated complex challenges while upholding her commitment to ethical leadership.

Napoleon Bonaparte: The military leader and emperor of France displayed unwavering self-discipline in his approach to leadership and strategy. His meticulous planning and adherence to principles of meritocracy and efficiency set him apart as a disciplined leader.

Mary Barra: As the CEO of General Motors, Mary Barra exhibited self-discipline by overseeing a massive company-wide recall while maintaining transparency and integrity. Her focus on safety and accountability exemplifies the discipline of ethical leadership.

Gandhi: Mahatma Gandhi's commitment to nonviolence, integrity, and ethical leadership showcased self-discipline at its core. His unwavering adherence to principles of truth and justice inspired a nation and led to transformative change.

These leaders, among many others, demonstrate that self-discipline is not a mere trait but a dynamic and essential quality for effective leadership. Their stories underscore the profound impact that self-discipline can have on an organization and its people.

Practical Steps to Cultivate Self-Discipline

Cultivating self-discipline is a journey that requires self-awareness and consistent effort. Here are practical steps to strengthen your self-discipline as a leader:

Identify Core Values: Clearly define your core values and principles to serve as a foundation for your decisions and actions.

Set Clear Goals: Establish clear and achievable goals that align with your values and long-term vision.

Develop Time Management Skills: Learn effective time management techniques to allocate your time and resources efficiently.

Practice Emotional Regulation: Develop strategies to manage and control your emotions in high-pressure situations.

Seek Feedback: Actively seek feedback from colleagues, mentors, and team members to improve your decision-making and behavior.

Reflect and Learn: Take time for self-reflection and learning from your experiences, both successes and failures.

Stay Accountable: Hold yourself accountable for your actions and decisions, and be transparent about your accountability to others.

Maintain Consistency: Consistently adhere to your values and principles in both small and significant decisions.

Practice Integrity: Uphold your commitment to honesty and ethical conduct in all interactions and decisions.

Stay Adaptable: Be open to adapting your approach and strategies based on feedback and changing circumstances.

The Enduring Legacy of Self-Discipline

Self-discipline emerges as the pillar that supports consistency, integrity, and ethical conduct. It is the discipline of self that enables leaders to stay true to their values, make sound decisions, and inspire trust in their teams and organizations. As you embark on your leadership journey, remember that self-discipline is not a rigid constraint but a source of strength and clarity—a compass that guides you toward excellence and enduring success. It is the key to consistency in leadership, paving the way for a brand of leadership marked by integrity, reliability, and unwavering commitment to what is right.

Chapter 5

Sustainability:
The Glue of Leadership

Sustainability emerges as the adhesive that binds together the diverse threads of character, values, and actions. It is the ability to perpetuate hard work, mental strength, and self-discipline consistently over the long term. Sustainability is not merely a buzzword or a fleeting concept; it is the enduring foundation upon which resilient and impactful leadership brands are constructed.

Understanding Sustainability in Leadership

Sustainability in leadership extends far beyond environmental concerns or corporate social responsibility—it encompasses the capacity of leaders to maintain their principles, values, and practices consistently over time. Sustainable leadership endures, remaining unwavering in the face of adversity, change, and external pressures.

At its core, sustainability in leadership is characterized by:

Consistency of Values: The unwavering commitment to core values and principles, regardless of external influences or challenges.

Long-Term Vision: A focus on long-term goals and enduring impact, rather than short-term gains or immediate results.

Adaptability: The ability to adjust strategies and approaches while staying true to foundational values.

Resilience: The capacity to rebound from setbacks, maintain momentum, and persist in the face of difficulties.

Legacy-Building: The intention to leave a lasting and positive imprint, shaping the organization or community for the better.

The Sustainability Mindset

Sustainability in leadership begins with the cultivation of a sustainability mindset—a way of thinking that prioritizes long-term impact and responsible stewardship. Leaders with a sustainability mindset view their roles as custodians of the future, embracing the responsibility to leave a positive legacy for generations to come.

Key elements of the sustainability mindset include:

Forward-Thinking: Leaders anticipate future challenges and opportunities, making decisions that consider the needs and well-being of future generations.

Systems Thinking: They recognize the interconnectedness of their actions and decisions within a broader ecosystem, considering the ripple effects of their choices.

Resource Stewardship: Leaders manage resources responsibly, minimizing waste, and seeking sustainable solutions.

Ethical Leadership: Ethical conduct is non-negotiable, as they understand that ethical lapses can have long-lasting negative consequences.

Resilience and Adaptability: Leaders embrace change and adversity as opportunities for growth and learning, fostering resilience and adaptability.

The Three Pillars
of Leadership Sustainability

Leadership sustainability rests upon three interrelated pillars, each reinforcing the others. These pillars are the embodiment of hard work, mental strength, and self-discipline, which, when practiced consistently, provide the base for overall leadership success.

Hard Work: Sustainable leadership requires a persistent commitment to putting in the time, effort, and sweat equity needed for continuous improvement. It's not about shortcuts or quick wins but the dedication to long-term growth and achievement.

Mental Strength: The resilience, determination, and adaptability that accompany mental strength are essential for leaders to weather storms, navigate change, and continue leading effectively, even when faced with significant challenges.

Self-Discipline: The discipline to consistently adhere to principles, values, and ethical standards is the linchpin of leadership sustainability. It ensures that leaders stay true to their course, make responsible decisions, and uphold their commitments.

The Sustainability Paradox

In the context of leadership, sustainability is a paradoxical concept. On one hand, it demands unwavering commitment to long-term goals and values. On the other hand, it requires adaptability and responsiveness to changing circumstances. Sustainable leaders must strike a delicate balance between constancy and flexibility.

This paradox often manifests in the tension between tradition and innovation, stability and change, and short-term results and long-term impact. Effective leaders navigate this balance, recognizing that sustainability does not equate to stagnation but rather to principled and adaptive progress.

Sustainability in Practice

Sustainable leadership is a lived experience, marked by a commitment to both enduring principles and continuous improvement. Here are practical ways in which sustainability manifests in leadership:

Long-Term Vision: Sustainable leaders articulate and communicate a compelling long-term vision that inspires and motivates their teams. This vision serves as a guiding star, helping everyone understand the organization's purpose and direction.

Values-Centered Leadership: Core values are not just words on a wall but guiding principles that drive decision-making and behavior. Sustainable leaders consistently uphold these values and hold themselves and others accountable to them.

Responsible Resource Management: Sustainability extends to resource management. Leaders must steward resources—financial, human, and environmental—with care, minimizing waste and maximizing efficiency.

Investment in Learning and Development: Sustainable leaders prioritize the growth and development of themselves and their teams. They invest in continuous learning, skill-building, and knowledge transfer to ensure a capable and adaptable workforce.

Resilient Decision-Making: Sustainable leaders make decisions that consider the long-term impact on the organization, community, and environment. They factor in potential risks and consequences, seeking to minimize negative outcomes.

Adaptive Leadership: In a rapidly changing world, sustainable leaders adapt to shifting circumstances, technologies, and market dynamics while maintaining their core values and principles.

Sustainability as a Legacy-Building Strategy

Leaders who prioritize sustainability are not just focused on the present; they are legacy builders. They understand that their actions and decisions today shape the future of their organizations and communities. A legacy of sustainability is marked by enduring positive impacts and a commitment to responsible leadership.

Legacy-building strategies of sustainable leaders include:

Mentorship and Succession Planning: Sustainable leaders invest in developing future leaders, ensuring the continuity of their organization's values and principles.

Community Engagement: They actively engage with and contribute to the well-being of their communities, leaving a positive mark beyond their immediate roles.

Environmental Responsibility: Sustainability-minded leaders consider the environmental impact of their actions and seek ways to reduce their organization's carbon footprint.

Ethical Governance: They establish ethical governance structures and practices that foster transparency, accountability, and responsible decision-making.

Social Responsibility: Sustainable leaders promote social responsibility by addressing societal issues, supporting charitable causes, and championing inclusivity and diversity.

Sustainable Leadership in Action

To better understand sustainable leadership in action, let's explore a notable example:

Patagonia: The outdoor clothing and gear company Patagonia is renowned for its commitment to sustainability. Founder Yvon Chouinard embedded sustainability into the company's DNA from its inception. Patagonia's sustainability initiatives include:

Environmental Stewardship: Patagonia prioritizes eco-friendly materials and sustainable manufacturing processes to minimize its environmental impact.

Social Responsibility: The company supports fair labor practices and advocates for workers' rights in its supply chain.

Worn Wear Program: Patagonia promotes the repair and reuse of its products through initiatives like the Worn Wear program, reducing waste and encouraging responsible consumption.

Activism: The company actively engages in environmental activism and advocacy, using its platform to address pressing environmental issues.

Patagonia's sustainability-focused leadership has not only earned it a loyal customer base but also set a benchmark for responsible business practices.

Practical Steps to Cultivate Sustainability in Leadership

Cultivating sustainability in leadership is an ongoing process that requires intentionality and commitment. Here are practical steps to help you build sustainable leadership:

Define Your Values: Clearly articulate your core values and principles, and ensure they align with your leadership style.

Set a Long-Term Vision: Develop a compelling long-term vision for your organization or team that inspires others and guides decision-making.

Practice Ethical Decision-Making: Prioritize ethical conduct in all decisions, even when it may seem challenging.

Invest in Learning: Commit to continuous learning and development for yourself and your team to stay adaptable and relevant.

Foster Resilience: Develop resilience strategies to bounce back from setbacks and maintain momentum in the face of adversity.

Engage with Your Community: Contribute to the well-being of your community through responsible actions and engagement.

Minimize Environmental Impact: Consider the environmental impact of your actions and seek sustainable solutions.

Promote Diversity and Inclusion: Create an inclusive environment that values diversity and promotes equal opportunities.

Mentor and Develop Others: Invest in the growth and development of emerging leaders to ensure a legacy of sustainability.

Reflect and Adapt: Regularly assess your leadership practices and adapt as needed to maintain alignment with your values and goals.

The Enduring Impact
of Sustainable Leadership

Sustainability stands as the glue that holds together the qualities of hard work, mental strength, and self-discipline. It is the commitment to enduring principles, values, and actions that enables leaders to weather storms, navigate change, and leave a lasting positive legacy. As you embark on your leadership journey, remember that sustainability is not a fleeting concept but a timeless commitment—a promise to lead with integrity, resilience, and a vision for a better future. It is the glue that binds great leaders to their enduring impact.

Chapter 6

Communication: The Leader's Voice

Communication has emerged as the vibrant thread that weaves together the aspirations, vision, and actions of a leader. It is the leader's voice, the medium through which ideas are articulated, connections are forged, and influence is wielded. Effective communication is not a mere skill; it is the lifeblood of leadership, empowering leaders to inspire, guide, and drive meaningful change.

The Power of Effective Communication

Effective communication in leadership is the ability to convey ideas, vision, expectations, and feedback clearly and persuasively. It is the foundation upon which trust, collaboration, and synergy are built within an organization. Leaders who master the art of effective communication become not only more influential but also more relatable, fostering a sense of unity and purpose among their teams.

At its core, effective communication in leadership encompasses:

Clarity: The ability to express ideas in a straightforward, concise, and easily understandable manner.

Authenticity: Communicating with sincerity and transparency, aligning words with actions.

Active Listening: Paying attention to others, seeking to understand their perspectives, and valuing their input.

Empathy: Understanding and acknowledging the feelings and concerns of others.

Influence: Persuading and inspiring others to take action or embrace a shared vision.

Communication as a Leadership Skill

Communication is often hailed as one of the most critical leadership skills, if not the most critical. Leaders who excel in communication can articulate their thoughts, engage their teams, and navigate complex situations with finesse. Effective communication is a skill that can be developed and refined over time, enhancing a leader's capacity to inspire and motivate.

The Three Dimensions of Effective Communication

Effective communication in leadership encompasses three interconnected dimensions, each serving a distinct purpose and contributing to a leader's overall communication prowess:

Verbal Communication: This dimension encompasses spoken and written language. It involves articulating ideas clearly, persuasively, and with impact. Verbal communication includes presentations, speeches, team meetings, written reports, and everyday conversations.

Non-Verbal Communication: Non-verbal communication encompasses body language, facial expressions, gestures, and tone of voice. It often conveys more about a leader's message than the words themselves. Leaders must be aware of their non-verbal cues and use them intentionally to reinforce their messages.

Listening Skills: Effective communication is not a one-way street; it involves active and empathetic listening. Leaders must pay attention to others, show interest in their perspectives, and ask clarifying questions. Listening skills are essential for building trust and understanding within teams.

The Role of Communication in Leadership

Communication plays multifaceted roles in leadership, each contributing to a leader's effectiveness and influence. Let's explore these roles in detail:

Vision Casting: Effective leaders use communication to cast a compelling vision for their organizations or teams. They paint a vivid picture of the future, inspiring others to share in their aspirations and goals.

Motivation and Inspiration: Leaders use their words to motivate and inspire their teams. They convey enthusiasm, determination, and belief in the team's abilities, instilling a sense of purpose and passion.

Alignment: Communication helps ensure that everyone within an organization or team is aligned with common goals and objectives. It clarifies expectations and provides direction.

Conflict Resolution: Leaders use communication to address conflicts and disagreements constructively. They facilitate open and honest discussions, seeking resolutions that benefit all parties.

Feedback and Development: Providing constructive feedback is a crucial aspect of leadership. Leaders use communication to help individuals grow, offering praise and constructive criticism as needed.

Decision-Making: Leaders involve others in the decision-making process through effective communication. They seek input, consider diverse perspectives, and communicate decisions clearly.

Change Management: In times of change, communication is vital. Leaders must convey the reasons for change, the intended outcomes, and the steps involved. They address concerns and provide reassurance.

The Art of Clarity in Communication

Clarity is the linchpin of effective communication. It ensures that the intended message is understood as intended. Leaders who communicate with clarity:

Use Simple Language: They avoid jargon and complex terminology, opting for plain, straightforward language.

Organize Information: They structure their messages logically, using headings, bullet points, and clear transitions.

Eliminate Ambiguity: They remove vagueness and ambiguity from their messages, leaving no room for misinterpretation.

Tailor the Message: They consider the audience and adapt their communication style and language to suit the recipient's level of understanding and preferences.

Provide Context: Leaders offer context to help others grasp the significance and relevance of their messages.

The Power of Authenticity

Authenticity in communication is the bridge that connects leaders to their teams. It involves being genuine, sincere, and transparent in one's communication. Authentic leaders:

Speak Honestly: They tell the truth, even when the message is challenging.

Align Words with Actions: Their words and actions are consistent, reinforcing their credibility.

Share Vulnerability: They are willing to admit mistakes and acknowledge their imperfections, fostering trust and relatability.

Express Empathy: Authentic leaders acknowledge the feelings and concerns of others, demonstrating empathy and compassion.

Listen Actively: They actively listen to others, valuing their perspectives and input.

The Role of Active Listening

Active listening is a cornerstone of effective communication. Leaders who excel in active listening:

Give Their Full Attention: They focus on the speaker, eliminating distractions and showing genuine interest.

Ask Open-Ended Questions: They encourage deeper discussions by asking questions that invite detailed responses.

Reflect and Paraphrase: They reflect on what they've heard, paraphrasing to ensure they've understood correctly.

Avoid Interruptions: Leaders refrain from interrupting, allowing the speaker to express their thoughts fully.

Empathize and Validate: They demonstrate empathy, acknowledging the speaker's emotions and validating their feelings.

Influence Through Persuasive Communication

Leaders often need to influence others to achieve goals and objectives. Persuasive communication is the art of convincing others to embrace a particular viewpoint or take specific actions. Leaders who excel in persuasive communication:

Understand Their Audience: They know their audience's needs, concerns, and motivations.

Build Credibility: They establish themselves as credible sources of information and expertise

Use Evidence and Logic: They support their arguments with compelling evidence and logical reasoning.

Appeal to Emotions: They connect with their audience emotionally, appealing to their values, aspirations, and emotions.

Engage in Storytelling: Leaders use stories and anecdotes to make their messages relatable and memorable.

Communication Challenges and Pitfalls

While effective communication is essential for leadership success, there are several common challenges and pitfalls that leaders must be aware of and mitigate:

Miscommunication: Messages may be misunderstood or misinterpreted, leading to confusion and misunderstandings.

Assumptions: Leaders may assume that others understand their perspective, leading to unspoken expectations and unaddressed concerns.

Overcommunication: Excessive communication can overwhelm teams and dilute the impact of important messages.

Lack of Feedback: Leaders who do not seek feedback may remain unaware of how their communication is perceived.

Failure to Adapt: Leaders who do not adapt their communication style to different audiences may struggle to connect effectively.

Practical Steps
to Enhance Communication Skills

Enhancing communication skills is an ongoing journey for leaders. Here are practical steps to improve your communication as a leader:

Reflect on Your Communication Style: Take time to assess your current communication style and its effectiveness.

Seek Feedback: Ask for feedback from colleagues, mentors, or coaches to identify areas for improvement.

Practice Active Listening: Develop active listening skills by consciously focusing on understanding others before responding.

Hone Clarity: Pay attention to the clarity of your messages, ensuring they are easy to understand.

Embrace Authenticity: Work on being authentic in your communication, aligning your words with your values.

Develop Persuasive Skills: Study persuasive communication techniques and practice them in your interactions.

Adapt to Your Audience: Tailor your communication style to suit the preferences and needs of your audience.

Use Storytelling: Learn the art of storytelling to make your messages more engaging and memorable.

Address Conflict Constructively: Develop conflict resolution skills to handle disagreements and disputes effectively.

Stay Informed: Continuously educate yourself on communication trends and best practices.

The Enduring Impact of Effective Communication

Communication is the lifeblood that sustains teams, organizations, and visions. It is the leader's voice, the conduit through which ideas are shared, trust is built, and influence is wielded. As you embark on your leadership journey, remember that effective communication is not just a skill but a force that empowers you to inspire, guide, and bring about meaningful change. It is the essence of leadership, the vibrant thread that connects leaders to their teams and propels them toward shared aspirations and success.

Chapter 7

Evaluation: The Path to Improvement

Evaluation serves as the compass that guides leaders toward continuous improvement and growth. It is the process of assessing one's performance, decisions, and actions to gain insights, make informed adjustments, and drive meaningful progress. Evaluation is not an end in itself but a means to elevate leadership to its highest potential, fostering resilience and adaptability while fortifying one's leadership brand.

The Essence of Evaluation in Leadership

Evaluation in leadership is the deliberate and systematic process of examining one's own performance, as well as the performance of teams and organizations, to identify strengths, weaknesses, opportunities, and threats. It involves gathering data, reflecting on outcomes, and using these insights to refine strategies, make informed decisions, and enhance leadership effectiveness.

At its core, evaluation in leadership embodies:

Self-Reflection: The practice of introspection and self-assessment to gain a deeper understanding of one's leadership style, strengths, and areas for improvement.

Performance Metrics: The use of objective measures, such as key performance indicators (KPIs) and benchmarks, to assess progress and achievements.

Feedback Mechanisms: The establishment of feedback loops that enable leaders to receive input from peers, mentors, colleagues, and team members.

Continuous Learning: A commitment to ongoing learning and development, with a focus on integrating lessons from past experiences.

Adaptability: The willingness and ability to adapt strategies, behaviors, and decisions based on evaluation findings.

The Role of Evaluation in Leadership

Evaluation serves several critical roles in leadership, each contributing to the leader's growth and the development of a high-performance culture:

Performance Improvement: Evaluation identifies areas of strength and areas in need of improvement, allowing leaders to refine their skills and approaches.

Accountability: Evaluation holds leaders accountable for their actions and decisions, ensuring that they take responsibility for both successes and setbacks.

Decision Enhancement: Leaders use evaluation to inform decision-making, relying on data and feedback to make informed choices.

Goal Achievement: Evaluation helps leaders track progress toward goals and adjust strategies to stay on course.

Team Development: Leaders use evaluation to provide constructive feedback to team members, fostering their growth and development.

Adaptation to Change: In a rapidly changing environment, evaluation enables leaders to adapt and pivot as needed.

The Evaluation Process in Leadership

The evaluation process in leadership typically follows a structured and iterative framework, which can vary in complexity depending on the scope and goals of evaluation efforts. Here is a simplified overview of the evaluation process:

Define Objectives: Clearly state the objectives and goals of the evaluation. What specific aspects of leadership or performance will be assessed?

Collect Data: Gather relevant data and information through various means, such as surveys, performance metrics, feedback sessions, and self-assessment.

Analyze Data: Carefully examine the collected data to identify patterns, trends, strengths, weaknesses, and areas for improvement.

Reflect and Interpret: Reflect on the findings and interpretations, considering the broader context and implications for leadership effectiveness.

Set Goals for Improvement: Based on the evaluation findings, establish clear and actionable goals for improvement. What specific changes or adjustments are needed?

Develop an Action Plan: Create a detailed action plan that outlines the steps, strategies, and resources required to achieve the improvement goals.

Implement Changes: Put the action plan into action, making the necessary changes to leadership approaches, behaviors, or strategies.

Monitor Progress: Continuously monitor progress toward the improvement goals, adjusting the action plan as needed.

Seek Feedback: Solicit feedback from peers, mentors, colleagues, and team members to gauge the effectiveness of the changes made.

Reflect and Adapt: Periodically revisit the evaluation process to assess the impact of changes and make further adjustments as necessary.

Self-Reflection: The Heart of Evaluation

Self-reflection is a cornerstone of effective evaluation in leadership. It involves pausing, introspecting, and examining one's thoughts, actions, and decisions with honesty and clarity. This internal dialogue, an essential aspect of The Expansive Methodology (TEM™), allows leaders to gain valuable insights into their performance, uncover areas for improvement, and foster personal growth. Here, we delve deeper into the significance of self-reflection, its integration into TEM™, and practical strategies to make it an integral part of your leadership journey.

The Power of Self-Reflection

Enhanced Self-Awareness:

Self-reflection cultivates self-awareness, a foundational element of effective leadership. It enables you to understand your strengths, weaknesses, values, and motivations.

Improved Decision-Making:

Through self-reflection, you gain a clearer perspective on your decision-making processes. You can identify biases, challenge assumptions, and make more informed choices.

Empathy and Emotional Intelligence:

As you reflect on your own experiences, you become more empathetic and attuned to the emotions and needs of others. This enhances your emotional intelligence, a critical trait in leadership.

Personal Growth and Adaptability:

Self-reflection is a vehicle for personal growth. It allows you to recognize areas where you can evolve and adapt, fostering continuous improvement.

TEM™ and Self-Reflection

In TEM™, self-reflection forms an integral part of the evaluation process, which, in turn, drives improvement and accountability.

Self-Reflective Evaluation:

TEM™ advocates for self-reflective evaluation, where leaders assess their own performance and behaviors. This mirrors the principles of self-discipline and accountability.

Alignment with Sustainability:

Sustainable leadership is rooted in self-reflection. It's the ongoing process of assessing one's impact and ensuring alignment with long-term goals and ethical conduct.

Aids in Communication:

Effective communication, another TEM™ pillar, is facilitated through self-reflection. Leaders who understand their communication styles and patterns can adapt and improve their interactions.

Practical Strategies
for Self-Reflection

Now, let's explore some practical strategies to embrace self-reflection as a vital component of your leadership journey within TEM™:

Designate Reflection Time:

Set aside dedicated time for self-reflection in your daily or weekly routine. Find a quiet space where you can think, ponder, and journal your thoughts.

Ask Provocative Questions:

Challenge yourself with thought-provoking questions. For example, "What did I learn from today's challenges?" or "How did my actions align with our organization's values?"

Journaling:

Maintain a journal to record your reflections, insights, and goals. Review your journal periodically to track your progress and identify recurring patterns.

Feedback Solicitation:

Seek feedback from peers, mentors, and team members. Their perspectives can provide valuable insights for self-reflection.

Set Specific Goals:

Establish clear and measurable goals for self-improvement. Regularly assess your progress toward these objectives.

Review Past Decisions:

Reflect on past decisions and their outcomes. What worked well, and what could have been done differently? This exercise enhances your decision-making skills.

Mindfulness Practices:

Incorporate mindfulness and meditation into your routine. These practices promote self-awareness and clarity of thought.

Peer Learning:

Engage in peer learning groups or discussions where you can share experiences, insights, and challenges. Peer perspectives can trigger valuable self-reflection.

Action Planning:

After self-reflection, create action plans for improvement. Identify specific steps and timelines for implementing changes based on your insights.

Embrace Failure as Learning:

View failures not as setbacks but as opportunities for growth. Reflect on what went wrong, what you learned, and how you can apply these lessons in the future.

Regular Check-Ins:

Schedule regular self-reflection check-ins in your calendar. Treat these appointments with the same importance as other commitments.

In the TEM™ framework, self-reflection is not a solitary endeavor; it's a shared commitment to personal and organizational growth. It's the compass that guides your journey towards becoming a more effective leader. By making self-reflection an integral part of your leadership approach, you foster continuous improvement, enhance accountability, and align your actions with the core principles of TEM™. Remember, self-reflection is not a passive exercise; it's an active pursuit of self-awareness and a powerful catalyst for positive change in your leadership journey.

Chapter 8

Accountability: Owning Your Leadership

Accountability is the bedrock upon which exceptional leadership is built. It's the unwavering commitment to taking responsibility for one's actions, decisions, and their consequences. In this chapter, we will explore the profound significance of accountability in leadership, the pillars that support it, and the transformative power it holds for leaders and their teams.

The Essence of Accountability in Leadership

Accountability in leadership is a multi-faceted concept that embodies responsibility, integrity, and transparency. It is the acknowledgement that leaders, regardless of their position or authority, are answerable for their actions and decisions. True accountability transcends mere compliance with rules and regulations; it is a personal and moral commitment to the principles that guide ethical leadership.

At its core, accountability in leadership encompasses:

Ownership of Actions: Leaders willingly embrace the consequences of their choices and actions, whether they lead to success or failure.

Transparency: Leaders communicate openly about their decisions, processes, and intentions, fostering trust and credibility among their team members.

Responsibility to Stakeholders: Leaders recognize their duty not only to their organizations but also to their employees, customers, and the broader community.

Adherence to Ethical Standards: Leaders uphold a strong moral compass, adhering to ethical principles even when faced with difficult choices.

Continuous Improvement: Accountable leaders are committed to self-reflection and growth, always seeking ways to enhance their leadership effectiveness.

The Role of Accountability in Leadership

Accountability is the linchpin that holds the leader's actions in check and ensures the alignment of leadership with the organization's mission and values. Its significance in leadership is manifold:

Trust Building: Accountability cultivates trust among team members, who feel assured that their leader will act in the best interests of the team and the organization.

Conflict Resolution: When conflicts arise, accountable leaders take ownership and work toward resolutions, minimizing disruptions and fostering a harmonious work environment.

Learning from Failure: Instead of assigning blame, accountable leaders view failure as an opportunity for growth. They analyze mistakes, identify lessons, and apply them to future endeavors.

Goal Achievement: Accountability drives leaders to set and achieve meaningful goals, inspiring their teams to strive for excellence.

Organizational Integrity: Accountable leaders set an example for ethical behavior, promoting a culture of integrity within the organization.

Employee Engagement: Teams led by accountable leaders tend to be more engaged, as employees feel valued and heard, contributing to higher morale and productivity.

The Accountability Framework in Leadership

Effective accountability in leadership is not arbitrary; it follows a structured framework that ensures clarity and consistency. This framework encompasses the following key elements:

Clear Expectations: Leaders must establish clear expectations and standards for themselves and their teams. These expectations should align with the organization's values and objectives.

Transparent Communication: Accountability thrives in an environment of open and transparent communication. Leaders should keep their teams informed about decisions, changes, and progress.

Responsibility Assignment: Leaders should clearly define roles and responsibilities within their teams, ensuring that each team member understands their part in achieving collective goals.

Performance Metrics: Metrics and key performance indicators (KPIs) provide quantifiable benchmarks against which performance can be evaluated. Leaders and team members should be aware of these metrics.

Feedback Loops: Regular feedback, both constructive and positive, is essential for accountability. Leaders should provide feedback to team members and be open to receiving feedback themselves.

Consequences and Rewards: Accountability is reinforced when there are consequences for failing to meet expectations and rewards for exceptional performance. Leaders should administer both fairly and consistently.

The Personal Accountability Journey

Personal accountability begins with introspection and the recognition that leadership entails not just privilege but also responsibility. Leaders must embark on a personal accountability journey that involves the following steps:

Self-Awareness: Leaders should have a deep understanding of their values, strengths, weaknesses, and leadership style. This self-awareness forms the foundation of personal accountability.

Goal Setting: Accountable leaders set clear and achievable goals that align with their personal values and the organization's mission.

Decision-Making: Leaders should make decisions that reflect their ethical principles and are in the best interests of their team and organization.

Ownership: When outcomes, whether positive or negative, result from their decisions, accountable leaders take full ownership and do not deflect blame onto others.

Adaptation: Personal accountability involves a commitment to learning and growth. Leaders should continuously adapt and improve their leadership approaches.

Accountability in Action: Real Stories

Real stories of leaders who have embraced accountability provide inspiration and practical insights. Let's explore a few of these narratives:

John Lewis (Late): The late civil rights icon, Congressman John Lewis, embodied accountability in his lifelong pursuit of justice and equality. From the front lines of the civil rights movement to the halls of Congress, Lewis held individuals and institutions accountable for discrimination and inequality. His unwavering dedication to accountability continues to inspire generations.

Indra Nooyi: As the former CEO of PepsiCo, Indra Nooyi exhibited exemplary accountability by prioritizing sustainability and diversity in the organization. She recognized the responsibility of a global corporation to contribute positively to society and took actions to reduce the company's environmental footprint.

Warren Buffett: The legendary investor and CEO of Berkshire Hathaway is renowned for his accountability in financial markets. He is known to openly admit his mistakes and share lessons learned, reinforcing the importance of taking responsibility for investment decisions.

These stories illustrate that accountability is not just a theoretical concept but a practical and essential aspect of leadership that can lead to remarkable achievements.

The Accountability Challenge

While accountability is a vital aspect of leadership, it is not without its challenges. Some common challenges that leaders may face in practicing accountability include:

Fear of Repercussions: Leaders may fear negative consequences, such as damage to their reputation or career, which can deter them from taking ownership of failures.

Blame-Shifting: It is tempting for leaders to shift blame onto others when things go wrong. This behavior erodes trust and undermines accountability.

Lack of Clarity: If expectations and roles are not clearly defined, leaders and team members may struggle to understand what they are accountable for.

Resistance to Feedback: Some leaders may resist feedback, viewing it as a threat to their authority or competence. This resistance can hinder personal growth and accountability.

Short-Term Focus: A focus on short-term results can lead to decisions that prioritize immediate gains over long-term accountability.

Overcoming Accountability Challenges

Leaders can overcome accountability challenges by adopting the following strategies:

Cultivate a Growth Mindset: Embrace failures as opportunities for growth and learning rather than as personal setbacks.

Lead by Example: Demonstrate accountability in your own actions and decisions, setting the standard for your team.

Encourage Open Communication: Foster a culture of open

and honest communication, where team members feel comfortable discussing challenges and providing feedback.

Define Expectations Clearly: Ensure that roles, responsibilities, and expectations are clearly defined to avoid confusion.

Seek Accountability Partners: Connect with mentors, peers, or accountability partners who can provide guidance and support in your leadership journey.

Focus on Long-Term Goals: Prioritize long-term goals and ethical principles over short-term gains, aligning your decisions with your values.

The Transformative Power of Accountability

Embracing accountability can lead to profound transformations in leadership and organizational culture:

Enhanced Trust: Accountable leaders build trust among team members, fostering strong relationships and collaboration.

Improved Problem-Solving: When leaders take ownership of issues, problems are addressed more effectively, leading to better solutions.

Innovation: A culture of accountability encourages experimentation and innovation, as leaders and team members are not afraid to take calculated risks.

Resilience: Accountable leaders bounce back from setbacks with resilience and determination, inspiring their teams to do the same.

Organizational Excellence: Accountability permeates the organization, leading to higher performance and a reputation for integrity.

Personal Fulfillment: Leaders who practice accountability often find greater personal fulfillment and a sense of purpose in their roles.

The Accountability Imperative

Accountability stands as a non-negotiable imperative. It is the force that drives leaders to excel, organizations to thrive, and societies to prosper. Through personal accountability and the establishment of accountability frameworks, leaders can navigate challenges, inspire trust, and forge a path toward lasting success. As you embark on your leadership journey, remember that accountability is not a burden but a privilege—one that empowers you to make a meaningful impact and leave a legacy of excellence.

Chapter 9

The TEM™ Approach in Action

In leadership, theories and principles abound, each offering its unique perspective on how to steer the ship toward success. Among these, The Expansive Methodology (TEM™) stands as a beacon—a practical and holistic framework that combines four fundamental character traits and personal philosophies, igniting positive productivity and propelling leaders to the zenith of their potential.

TEM™, born from a bottom-up approach, asserts that hard work, mental strength, self-discipline, and sustainability are the cornerstones of successful leadership. In this chapter, we delve deep into the practical application of TEM™, exploring how these traits and philosophies come together to create a dynamic and transformative leadership approach.

Understanding the TEM™ Approach

Before we plunge into the TEM™ approach in action, let's briefly recap the four pillars that underpin this methodology:

Hard Work: The unwavering dedication to invest maximum effort, time, and sweat equity to improve and excel in one's role. Hard work transcends innate talent, emphasizing the importance of sustained effort.

Mental Strength: The ability to endure and persist in the face of adversity, challenges, and demanding situations. Mental strength empowers leaders to push through tough times, showing up even when the inclination is to give in.

Self-Discipline: The practice of consistently doing the right thing at the right time and place. It involves conditioning one's thought process, performing tasks as required, evaluating oneself, and having the discipline to improve based on that evaluation.

Sustainability: The capacity to sustain hard work, mental strength, and self-discipline over the long term. Sustainability is the foundation upon which true leadership is built, as it enables leaders to weather storms and continue on the path to success.

TEM™ in Action: The Synergy of Pillars

Now, let's explore how these pillars come to life in the daily practices and behaviors of successful leaders.

Hard Work: The Unrelenting Pursuit of Excellence

Hard work is the fuel that propels leaders forward, enabling them to achieve their goals and exceed expectations. Here's how hard work manifests in leadership:

Setting Ambitious Goals: Leaders who embrace hard work set ambitious goals for themselves and their teams. These goals serve as a driving force, motivating them to invest maximum effort.

Continuous Learning: Hard Working leaders are lifelong learners. They seek out opportunities for growth, whether through formal education, mentorship, or self-directed study.

Leading by Example: A hardworking leader sets the tone for the entire team. When team members see their leader consistently putting in the effort, it inspires them to do the same.

Diligent Preparation: Hard work involves diligent preparation for challenges and tasks. Leaders who put in the time to prepare are better equipped to handle unexpected obstacles.

Resilience in Adversity: When faced with setbacks or obstacles, hard working leaders do not back down. They persevere, using their determination and effort to overcome challenges.

Mental Strength: The Power to Overcome

Mental strength is the fortitude that empowers leaders to navigate the often turbulent waters of leadership. Here's how mental strength plays out in leadership:

Embracing Challenges: Mentally strong leaders do not shy away from challenges; they embrace them as opportunities for growth.

Remaining Calm Under Pressure: In high-pressure situations, mental strength allows leaders to stay composed, make rational decisions, and provide guidance to their teams.

Handling Criticism: Leaders with mental strength can accept constructive criticism without becoming defensive. They view feedback as a valuable tool for improvement.

Positive Mindset: Mental strength is closely tied to a positive mindset. Leaders who cultivate optimism and resilience are better equipped to inspire and motivate their teams.

Grit and Tenacity: Leaders with mental strength exhibit grit and tenacity. They keep pushing forward, even when the path is difficult or uncertain.

Self-Discipline: The Key to Consistency

Self-discipline is the cornerstone of consistency in leadership. It ensures that leaders consistently perform at their best. Here's how self-discipline manifests in leadership:

Consistent Execution: Self-disciplined leaders consistently execute their tasks and responsibilities with precision and reliability.

Adherence to Values: Leaders with self-discipline adhere to their core values and principles, even when faced with ethical dilemmas.

Time Management: Self-discipline extends to time management. Leaders prioritize their tasks and allocate their time effectively to achieve their goals.

Accountability to Self: Self-disciplined leaders hold themselves accountable. They recognize that they are responsible for their actions and decisions.

Continuous Improvement: Self-discipline drives leaders to continually seek opportunities for improvement and growth. They are not content with the status quo.

Sustainability: The Long-Term Perspective

Sustainability is the glue that holds the pillars of TEM™ together, ensuring that leadership excellence endures over time. Here's how sustainability is woven into leadership:

Long-Term Vision: Sustainable leaders have a long-term vision for their organizations and teams. They make decisions that align with this vision.

Resilience in the Face of Setbacks: Sustainable leadership involves bouncing back from setbacks and maintaining a forward-looking perspective.

Cultivating Future Leaders: Sustainable leaders invest in the development of future leaders, ensuring that their legacy of excellence continues.

Balancing Well-Being: Sustainability extends to the well-being of leaders themselves. Sustainable leaders prioritize self-care and work-life balance to maintain their effectiveness over time.

Adapting to Change: Sustainable leaders are adaptable. They embrace change and are not deterred by the evolving landscape of leadership.

The TEM™ Approach in Leadership Practices

To fully grasp the impact of TEM™ in leadership, let's examine how these four pillars are integrated into leadership practices across different domains:

TEM™ in Business Leadership

In the world of business, TEM™ plays a pivotal role in driving success. Business leaders who embody the TEM™ approach:

1. Set aggressive goals for their organizations and lead by example

in putting in the hard work required to achieve them.

2. Navigate the complex and competitive landscape with mental strength, making sound decisions under pressure.

3. Uphold self-discipline by adhering to ethical standards, managing resources efficiently, and consistently delivering results.

4. Ensure the sustainability of their businesses by maintaining a long-term vision, adapting to market changes, and nurturing a culture of innovation.

TEM™ in Team Leadership

Leaders who manage teams benefit greatly from TEM™:

1. Hard work motivates team members to excel, and leaders who work alongside their teams build camaraderie and trust.

2. Mental strength helps leaders remain composed during team challenges and provide the support and guidance needed.

3. Self-discipline is essential for setting clear expectations, managing team resources effectively, and holding team members accountable.

4. Sustainability ensures that the team's success is not short-lived, with leaders fostering an environment of continuous learning and improvement.

TEM™ in Community Leadership

Community leaders who embrace TEM™ create a positive impact:

1. Hard work in community leadership involves tireless advocacy and effort toward achieving community goals.

2. Mental strength allows leaders to persevere in the face of complex social issues and navigate the challenges of community development.

3. Self-discipline is crucial for maintaining transparency and accountability in community initiatives.

4. Sustainability means ensuring the long-term well-being and progress of the community, even as it evolves.

TEM™ in Personal Leadership

At the core of personal leadership, TEM™ offers a compass for self-improvement:

1. Hard work drives individuals to continuously strive for personal growth and development.

2. Mental strength helps individuals face life's challenges with resilience and a positive outlook.

3. Self-discipline allows individuals to set and achieve personal goals and maintain healthy habits.

4. Sustainability ensures that personal leadership endures, leading to a fulfilling and purpose-driven life.

Case Studies: TEM™ in Action

Let's delve into real-world case studies that exemplify how TEM™ has transformed leaders and organizations.

Case Study 1: Mary's Remarkable Journey

Mary, a mid-level manager at a technology company, found herself at a crossroads in her career. She felt stuck and lacked motivation. It was during a leadership development program that she encountered TEM™. Inspired by the philosophy, Mary decided to apply the four pillars to her leadership journey.

Hard Work: Mary set ambitious goals for her team and herself, focusing on innovation and efficiency. She put in extra hours to lead by example, and her team responded with increased dedication and enthusiasm.

Mental Strength: When a major project faced unexpected challenges, Mary remained steadfast. She communicated transparently with her team, inspiring them to tackle the issues head-on. Her mental strength played a crucial role in turning the project around.

Self-Discipline: Mary instilled discipline in her team by setting clear expectations and adhering to project timelines. She implemented feedback loops to ensure continuous improvement. Her self-discipline was reflected in her meticulous planning and execution.

Sustainability: Mary's long-term vision included nurturing talent within her team. She invested in coaching and mentoring team members, preparing them for leadership roles. Her sustainable approach ensured the team's ongoing success.

As a result of her TEM™-inspired leadership, Mary not only achieved her career goals but also became a role model within her organization, inspiring others to adopt the TEM™ approach.

Case Study 2: The TEM™ Driven Nonprofit

A nonprofit organization dedicated to environmental conservation faced the challenge of declining donor support and increasing competition for funding. The organization's leadership decided to adopt TEM™ to revitalize their mission.

Hard Work: The organization set ambitious fundraising goals and worked tirelessly to engage donors and supporters. Their commitment to hard work led to increased funding and support.

Mental Strength: When faced with skepticism and obstacles in their conservation efforts, the leadership remained resolute. They communicated the urgency of their mission with unwavering determination, inspiring volunteers and staff.

Self-Discipline: The organization implemented rigorous financial management practices and accountability mechanisms to ensure that donor funds were used effectively. They also conducted regular self-assessments to identify areas for improvement.

Sustainability: The leadership embraced a long-term vision, focusing on the preservation of natural resources for future generations. They engaged with local communities and schools to promote sustainability and environmental awareness.

By applying TEM™ principles, the nonprofit not only secured its mission but also thrived, expanding its reach and impact on conservation efforts.

Implementing TEM™ in Your Leadership Journey

As you embark on your leadership journey, consider how you can integrate TEM™ principles into your approach:

Self-Assessment: Reflect on your leadership style and identify areas where you can apply the pillars of TEM™.

Goal Setting: Establish clear and ambitious goals for yourself and your organization, aligning them with TEM™ principles.

Action Plan: Create a plan that outlines how you will put hard work, mental strength, self-discipline, and sustainability into practice.

Team Engagement: Inspire and engage your team by embodying TEM™ principles and encouraging them to do the same.

Feedback and Adaptation: Continuously assess your progress, seek feedback, and adapt your leadership approach to align with TEM™.

Mentorship: Seek mentors or role models who exemplify TEM™ principles and learn from their experiences.

Inspiration: Draw inspiration from TEM™ success stories and case studies to fuel your own leadership journey.

Incorporating TEM™ into your leadership approach can lead to transformational growth, both for yourself and for those you lead. It's a journey that not only fosters personal and professional development but also propels organizations and communities toward greater success and impact. As you apply the principles of hard work, mental strength, self-discipline, and sustainability, you'll find that the TEM™ approach has the power to elevate your leadership to unprecedented heights.

Chapter 10

TEM™ in Self Leadership Context

The self serves as both the starting point and the driving force. The application of The Expansive Methodology (TEM™) within the context of self-leadership is an indispensable foundation upon which all other leadership endeavors are built. In this chapter, we delve into the profound significance of self-context within TEM™, exploring how self-awareness, self-mastery, and self-growth are intertwined with the four pillars of hard work, mental strength, self-discipline, and sustainability.

The Self as the Epicenter of Leadership

Leadership, at its essence, begins with the self. Effective leaders are not only aware of their strengths and weaknesses but are also capable of leveraging their self-awareness to inspire and guide others. In this self-context, TEM™ becomes a personal compass for leaders to navigate the complexities of their roles.

Self-Awareness: The Starting Point

Self-awareness is the cornerstone of effective leadership. It entails a deep understanding of one's values, beliefs, strengths, weaknesses, and the impact one has on others. In the TEM™ framework, self-awareness is the first step in the journey of self-context:

Understanding Values: Self-aware leaders are in touch with their core values and principles. They know what they stand for and align their actions with these values.

Embracing Strengths: Leaders recognize and embrace their strengths. They leverage these strengths to drive their leadership efforts and create a positive impact.

Acknowledging Weaknesses: Self-awareness also involves acknowledging areas where improvement is needed. Leaders are open to feedback and eager to address their weaknesses.

Empathy and Emotional Intelligence: Self-aware leaders possess empathy and emotional intelligence. They understand the emotions of others and use this understanding to build strong relationships.

Impact on Others: Leaders are mindful of the impact they have on their teams and organizations. They strive to be positive role models and inspire others through their actions.

Self-awareness, in the TEM™ context, serves as the foundation upon which the other pillars of hard work, mental strength, self-discipline, and sustainability are built. It guides leaders in aligning their efforts with their authentic selves and in setting meaningful goals.

Self-Mastery: The Path to Excellence

Self-mastery is the process of gaining control over one's thoughts, emotions, and actions. It empowers leaders to lead from a place of inner strength and authenticity:

Emotional Regulation: Self-mastery allows leaders to regulate their emotions effectively. They remain composed and focused even in challenging situations.

Resilience: Leaders with self-mastery bounce back from setbacks with resilience and determination. They view failures as opportunities for growth.

Decision-Making: Self-mastery enhances decision-making. Leaders make well-considered choices that align with their values and long-term vision.

Stress Management: Leaders practice stress management techniques to maintain their well-being and effectiveness. They prioritize self-care to sustain their leadership journey.

Conflict Resolution: Self-mastery equips leaders with the skills to navigate conflicts and disagreements constructively. They seek win-win solutions that benefit all parties.

Self-mastery within the TEM™ framework ensures that leaders are not driven solely by external pressures or circumstances. Instead, they draw from their internal reservoirs of strength and wisdom to lead with clarity and purpose.

Self-Growth: The Continuous Journey

Leaders who embrace self-growth recognize that leadership is an evolving journey. They are committed to ongoing learning, improvement, and personal development:

Continuous Learning: Self-growth involves a commitment to continuous learning. Leaders seek out opportunities to expand their knowledge and skills.

Adaptation: Leaders are adaptable and open to change. They embrace new ideas and innovations, staying relevant in an ever-evolving world.

Feedback and Reflection: Self-growth requires leaders to solicit feedback and engage in reflective practices. They use feedback as a tool for improvement and self-assessment.

Mentorship and Coaching: Leaders often seek mentorship or coaching to accelerate their growth. They learn from the experiences of others and apply those lessons to their leadership.

Purpose-Driven Leadership: Self-growth leads to purpose-driven leadership. Leaders discover their unique mission and vision, guiding their actions and decisions.

In the TEM™ framework, self-growth is not a destination but a continuous journey. It aligns with the sustainability pillar, ensuring that leaders remain effective and relevant over time.

TEM™ in Self-Context: A Holistic Approach

Now, let's explore how the four pillars of TEM™—hard work, mental strength, self-discipline, and sustainability—are interwoven within the context of self-leadership:

Hard Work in Self-Context

Hard work within self-context is about the relentless pursuit of self-improvement:

Setting Personal Goals: Leaders set ambitious personal development goals, striving to become the best version of themselves.

Commitment to Learning: They invest time and effort in acquiring new knowledge and skills, recognizing that self-improvement is an ongoing process.

Leading by Example: Hardworking self-leaders lead by example, inspiring others through their dedication to growth.

Overcoming Personal Challenges: In the face of personal challenges or setbacks, they apply mental strength to persevere and continue their growth journey.

Resilience: They view self-improvement as a long-term endeavor, displaying the sustainability pillar by sustaining their commitment to growth over time.

Mental Strength in Self-Context

Mental strength in self-context is the inner fortitude to overcome personal obstacles and maintain a positive mindset:

Facing Personal Challenges: Self-leaders with mental strength face personal challenges with resilience and a problem-solving attitude.

Optimism: They cultivate optimism and a growth mindset, believing in their capacity to improve and adapt.

Self-Reflection: Mental strength includes self-reflection, as leaders assess their thoughts and emotions to make constructive decisions.

Emotional Intelligence: Leaders with mental strength also possess emotional intelligence, allowing them to navigate their own emotions and relate to others effectively.

Sustaining Personal Growth: Mental strength sustains personal growth by enabling leaders to persevere through the inevitable ups and downs of the self-improvement journey.

Self-Discipline in Self-Context

Self-discipline in self-context involves maintaining a structured and purposeful approach to personal development:

Personal Routines: Leaders establish routines that support their growth, ensuring that they consistently allocate time to self-improvement.

Goal Alignment: Self-disciplined self-leaders align their personal goals with their core values, ensuring that their growth efforts are purposeful.

Accountability to Self: They hold themselves accountable for their personal development, recognizing that self-discipline begins with personal responsibility.

Feedback and Adaptation: Self-discipline involves seeking feedback on personal growth efforts and adapting as needed to stay on course.

Sustainability of Self-Improvement: Self-discipline ensures the sustainability of personal growth, as leaders consistently invest in their development.

Sustainability in Self-Context

Sustainability in self-context is about maintaining a long-term perspective on personal growth:

Long-Term Vision: Leaders with sustainability in mind have a clear long-term vision for their personal development, setting them on a path of continuous improvement.

Resilience in Self-Growth: They bounce back from personal setbacks and continue their growth journey, demonstrating resilience.

Cultivating Future Self-Leaders: Sustainable self-leaders also mentor and support others in their personal growth, fostering a culture of continuous improvement.

Adapting to Personal Change: They embrace personal change and evolution, recognizing that self-improvement is an ever-evolving process.

Balancing Well-Being: Sustainability involves balancing personal well-being to ensure that growth efforts enhance overall quality of life.

Case Study: Sarah's Journey of Self-Context Leadership

To illustrate TEM™ in self-context, let's explore the journey of Sarah, a mid-level manager in a fast-paced tech company:

Self-Awareness: Sarah begins her leadership journey by developing self-awareness. She conducts a thorough assessment of her strengths and weaknesses. She recognizes that she can be impatient with team members and tends to micromanage tasks due to her perfectionist tendencies.

Self-Mastery: Sarah takes steps to master her self-awareness. She practices mindfulness techniques to control her impatience and seeks stress-management strategies to overcome perfectionism. She develops emotional intelligence, allowing her to connect with her team members on a deeper level and understand their individual needs and motivations.

Self-Growth: Sarah's commitment to self-growth drives her to continuously seek opportunities for improvement. She enrolls in leadership workshops and seeks out a mentor within the company who provides guidance and feedback. She reflects on her experiences and learns from her mistakes, using them as stepping stones for growth.

TEM™ in Self-Context

Hard Work in Self-Context: Sarah sets ambitious personal development goals, such as improving her communication skills and fostering a more collaborative work environment. She dedicates extra hours to self-improvement, reading books on effective leadership and communication, and actively seeking feedback from her team members.

Mental Strength in Self-Context: Sarah faces personal challenges head-on, using her mental strength to persevere through difficult moments. She maintains a positive outlook, believing that her continuous growth will benefit both herself and her team. Her self-reflection helps her manage her emotions and make rational decisions.

Self-Discipline in Self-Context: Sarah establishes a structured daily routine that includes time for self-improvement activities. She aligns her personal goals with her core values, ensuring that her growth efforts are purposeful and meaningful. She holds herself accountable for her personal development, tracking her progress and making adjustments as needed.

Sustainability in Self-Context: Sarah maintains a long-term vision for her personal growth. She understands that self-improvement is an ongoing journey and remains resilient in the face of setbacks. She also mentors a junior team member, sharing her experiences and insights to foster a culture of continuous improvement within the organization.

Through her dedication to self-awareness, self-mastery, self-growth, and the integration of TEM™ principles, Sarah transforms into a more effective leader. Her improved communication and leadership skills not only benefit her career but also create a more collaborative and productive work environment for her team.

Implementing TEM™ in Self-Context

As you embark on your own journey of self-leadership within the TEM™ framework, consider the following steps:

Self-Assessment: Begin by conducting a thorough self-assessment to understand your values, strengths, weaknesses, and impact on others.

Goal Setting: Establish personal development goals that align with your core values and long-term vision.

Action Plan: Create a structured plan for achieving your goals, allocating time and resources to your self-improvement efforts.

Self-Mastery: Practice emotional regulation, resilience, and stress management to enhance your self-mastery.

Continuous Learning: Commit to ongoing learning and seek opportunities for personal growth and development.

Feedback and Reflection: Solicit feedback from mentors, peers, and team members to assess your progress and adapt your approach.

Mentorship: Consider seeking a mentor or coach who can provide guidance and support on your self-leadership journey.

Inspiration: Draw inspiration from the TEM™ principles and success stories of leaders who have applied them in self-context.

By integrating TEM™ into your self-leadership approach, you can enhance your self-awareness, master your emotions and actions, and embark on a continuous journey of personal growth and improvement. In doing so, you not only elevate your own leadership but also inspire and empower those you lead to follow a similar path of self-discovery and excellence. Remember that self-leadership within the TEM™ framework is not a destination but a lifelong journey of becoming the best version of yourself as a leader and as an individual.

Chapter 11

TEM™ in One-to-One Leadership Context

One-to-one interactions serve as the threads that bind leaders to their teams, peers, and colleagues. The application of The Expansive Methodology (TEM™) in the one-to-one context is a pivotal element of effective leadership, as it shapes the quality of relationships, fosters trust, and catalyzes collaboration. In this chapter, we delve into the profound significance of one-to-one interactions within the TEM™ framework, exploring how the four pillars of hard work, mental strength, self-discipline, and sustainability are woven into these critical exchanges.

The Crucial Nature of One-to-One Interactions

Leadership is, at its core, a relational endeavor. The ability to connect with individuals on a personal level, understand their needs, and inspire their best efforts is a hallmark of great leadership. One-to-one interactions provide a unique opportunity for leaders to influence, mentor, and empower those they engage with.

In the TEM™ framework, these interactions are seen as a microcosm of leadership, where the principles of hard work, mental strength, self-discipline, and sustainability are put into practice at an individual level. Let's explore how each of these pillars manifests in the one-to-one context.

Hard Work: The Foundation of Trust

Hard work in one-to-one interactions goes beyond the mere completion of tasks. It involves the dedication to invest time, effort, and attention in building and nurturing relationships. Here's how hard work manifests in one-to-one context:

Active Listening: Leaders who work hard in one-to-one interactions are active listeners. They devote their full attention to the other person, seeking to understand their perspectives and needs.

Preparation: Hardworking leaders come prepared for one-to-one meetings. They do their homework, gather relevant information, and formulate thoughtful questions and responses.

Follow-Up: After one-to-one interactions, they follow up on commitments and action items promptly. This demonstrates reliability and respect for the other person's time and expectations.

Empathy: Leaders who work hard in one-to-one interactions demonstrate empathy by acknowledging the emotions and concerns of the other person. They make an effort to connect on a human level.

Investment in Growth: Hardworking leaders view one-to-one interactions as opportunities for mutual growth. They provide constructive feedback, guidance, and mentorship to support the development of others.

Hard work in one-to-one interactions serves as the foundation of trust and respect. It signals to the other person that their thoughts, opinions, and well-being are valued.

Mental Strength: Navigating Challenges

Mental strength in one-to-one interactions empowers leaders to navigate challenges, conflicts, and difficult conversations with poise and effectiveness. Here's how mental strength plays out in this context:

Conflict Resolution: Leaders with mental strength approach conflicts in a constructive manner. They remain calm and composed, seeking win-win solutions and maintaining open lines of communication.

Difficult Feedback: When providing feedback, they do so with empathy and a growth mindset. They offer constructive criticism while highlighting areas for improvement.

Resilience: Mental strength enables leaders to bounce back from challenging one-to-one interactions. They do not let setbacks deter them from future engagements.

Emotional Intelligence: Leaders with mental strength exhibit emotional intelligence by recognizing and managing their own emotions and understanding the emotions of others.

Courageous Conversations: They are not afraid to engage in courageous conversations, addressing sensitive topics with authenticity and transparency.

Mental strength in one-to-one interactions fosters an environment of trust and psychological safety. It allows individuals to express themselves openly and honestly, knowing that their concerns will be heard and respected.

Self-Discipline: Consistency in Communication

Self-discipline in one-to-one interactions ensures consistency, reliability, and integrity in communication. Here's how self-discipline is manifested in this context:

Consistency: Self-disciplined leaders maintain consistency in their communication. They set clear expectations for regular one-to-one meetings and adhere to the established schedule.

Preparation: Before one-to-one interactions, they prepare agendas or discussion points to ensure that the time is used productively and that important topics are covered.

Adherence to Values: Self-discipline extends to adhering to core values and principles. Leaders prioritize ethical communication and respect for the other person's perspective.

Accountability: Self-disciplined leaders hold themselves accountable for their words and actions in one-to-one interactions. They do what they say they will do and take ownership of any commitments made.

Feedback Delivery: They deliver feedback with tact and diplomacy, focusing on specific behaviors and outcomes rather than making personal judgments.

Self-discipline in one-to-one interactions builds trust and credibility. It ensures that communication is reliable, respectful, and aligned with the leader's values and the organization's culture.

Sustainability: Nurturing Relationships

Sustainability in one-to-one interactions involves nurturing relationships over the long term, ensuring that they remain healthy and mutually beneficial. Here's how sustainability is expressed in this context:

Long-Term Perspective: Leaders with sustainability in mind view one-to-one interactions as part of a long-term relationship-building process. They consider the future impact of their actions and words.

Respectful Engagement: They engage with others respectfully, even in challenging situations. They are mindful of the potential long-term consequences of their interactions.

Cultivating Trust: Sustainable leaders prioritize trust as a foundational element of relationships. They consistently demonstrate trustworthiness and reliability.

Feedback Loop: They establish a feedback loop in one-to-one interactions, encouraging the other person to share their thoughts, concerns, and feedback. This ensures that the relationship remains responsive to changing needs.

Adaptation: Sustainable leaders are adaptable in their communication styles and approaches. They recognize that individuals and relationships evolve, and they adjust their interactions accordingly.

Sustainability in one-to-one interactions ensures that relationships endure, thrive, and contribute positively to the leader's effectiveness and the overall well-being of individuals and teams.

Case Study: John's Approach to One-to-One Context Leadership

John, a senior manager in a healthcare organization, exemplifies the application of TEM™ in one-to-one interactions. His approach to leadership within this context showcases the four pillars in action:

Hard Work: John actively listens to his team members during one-to-one meetings, creating a space for open and honest communication. He invests time in understanding their challenges and aspirations, demonstrating his commitment to their well-being and growth. John also sets aside time for regular one-to-one meetings, prioritizing these interactions as essential to building strong relationships.

Mental Strength: When conflicts arise within his team, John approaches them with mental strength. He remains composed and seeks to understand the underlying issues. He encourages team members to share their perspectives and emotions, fostering a climate of trust. John's ability to navigate difficult conversations with empathy and resilience contributes to a harmonious and collaborative work environment.

Self-Discipline: John maintains self-discipline in his one-to-one interactions by adhering to a consistent schedule. He prepares agendas for each meeting, ensuring that topics are addressed systematically. His communication is characterized by ethical conduct, and he holds himself accountable for any commitments made during these interactions. Team members appreciate his reliability and integrity.

Sustainability: John takes a long-term view of his relationships with team members. He focuses on nurturing trust and respect in each interaction, recognizing that these qualities are foundational to sustainable relationships. John actively seeks feedback from team members and adjusts his leadership approach to meet their evolving needs. As a result, his relationships with team members remain robust and continue to contribute to the organization's success.

John's leadership within the one-to-one context demonstrates the profound impact of TEM™ principles. His hard work, mental strength, self-discipline, and sustainability in these interactions not only strengthen relationships but also drive team engagement and performance.

Implementing TEM™
in One-to-One Context

To incorporate TEM™ principles into your one-to-one interactions, consider the following steps:

Prioritize One-to-One Time: Allocate dedicated time for one-to-one interactions with team members, peers, and colleagues. Make these interactions a priority in your schedule.

Active Listening: Practice active listening by giving your full attention to the other person. Seek to understand their perspectives and needs before responding.

Preparation: Prepare for one-to-one interactions by setting clear agendas or discussion points. Ensure that the meeting is productive and focused.

Conflict Resolution: Approach conflicts and difficult conversations with a mindset of seeking constructive solutions. Focus on open communication and understanding.

Consistency: Maintain consistency in your communication and engagement. Keep your commitments and adhere to established schedules for one-to-one meetings.

Ethical Conduct: Ensure that your interactions align with your core values and ethical standards. Uphold integrity and respect in your communication.

Trust Building: Prioritize trust as a foundational element of one-to-one interactions. Demonstrate trustworthiness and reliability in your engagements.

Feedback Loop: Establish a feedback loop in your interactions, inviting others to share their thoughts and concerns. Use feedback as a tool for continuous improvement.

Adaptation: Be adaptable in your communication styles and approaches. Recognize that relationships evolve, and adjust your interactions accordingly.

By integrating these TEM™ principles into your one-to-one interactions, you can cultivate strong and enduring relationships, foster trust, and drive collaboration and effectiveness within your team and organization. One-to-one interactions, when guided by the TEM™ framework, become a powerful catalyst for leadership growth and success.

Chapter 12

TEM™ in
Team Leadership Context

The team serves as the dynamic core, where the principles of The Expansive Methodology (TEM™) are applied in a collective context. Effective leadership within the team context is essential for achieving organizational goals, fostering collaboration, and nurturing individual growth. In this chapter, we explore how the four pillars of hard work, mental strength, self-discipline, and sustainability manifest within the team context, shaping leadership into a force that propels teams to success.

The Vital Role of Team Leadership

Leadership in the team context is the crucible where vision becomes reality, and goals are transformed into achievements. It's where the synergy of individual talents and efforts is harnessed to drive collective progress. Effective team leadership is characterized by the ability to inspire, motivate, and align team members toward a common purpose.

In the TEM™ framework, the team context is a fertile ground for the four pillars to flourish, guiding leaders to create an environment where hard work, mental strength, self-discipline, and sustainability are not just principles but lived experiences.

Hard Work: Fostering a Culture of Dedication

Hard work in the team context extends beyond individual effort; it encompasses the cultivation of a culture where dedication and diligence are shared values. Here's how hard work is manifested in team leadership:

Setting the Example: Leaders who embody hard work inspire their team members by setting a personal example of dedication. They consistently put in the effort required to achieve team goals.

Clear Expectations: They establish clear expectations for the level of effort and commitment expected from each team member. This clarity encourages a shared sense of responsibility.

Recognition and Rewards: Leaders recognize and reward hard work within the team. Celebrating achievements and acknowledging exceptional effort reinforces the culture of dedication.

Conflict Resolution: When conflicts arise within the team, hardworking leaders address them promptly and constructively. They ensure that conflicts do not hinder progress or erode team cohesion.

Continuous Improvement: Leaders who value hard work prioritize continuous improvement. They encourage team members to seek opportunities for growth and excellence.

In the team context, hard work serves as the bedrock upon which trust and collaboration are built. It fosters a sense of collective responsibility and a shared commitment to achieving common goals.

Mental Strength: Navigating Challenges Together

Mental strength within the team context is about equipping both leaders and team members with the resilience and adaptability needed to navigate challenges collectively. Here's how mental strength is expressed in team leadership:

Emotional Resilience: Leaders with mental strength maintain emotional resilience during times of adversity. They provide a stabilizing presence for their team, helping them weather storms with grace.

Team Support: They encourage open communication within the team, allowing team members to express their concerns and emotions. This promotes psychological safety and trust.

Problem Solving: Leaders with mental strength approach challenges as opportunities for problem-solving. They engage the collective intelligence of the team to find innovative solutions.

Positive Mindset: They cultivate a positive mindset within the team, emphasizing the potential for growth and learning even in difficult circumstances.

Conflict Transformation: Mental strength enables leaders to transform conflicts into opportunities for growth and strengthened relationships. They guide the team toward constructive dialogue and resolution.

Mental strength in team leadership helps teams remain resilient, adaptable, and united in the face of challenges. It fosters a culture where team members support one another and work cohesively to overcome obstacles.

Self-Discipline: Creating a Structure for Success

Self-discipline in the team context involves the establishment of a structured and purposeful environment that facilitates collaboration and goal attainment. Here's how self-discipline is practiced in team leadership:

Goal Alignment: Leaders align team goals with the organization's mission and vision. They ensure that each team member understands their role in achieving these goals.

Effective Communication: Self-disciplined leaders prioritize effective communication within the team. They establish channels for sharing information, updates, and feedback.

Role Clarity: Team members are provided with clear role descriptions and responsibilities. Self-disciplined leaders ensure that everyone knows what is expected of them.

Accountability: Leaders hold team members accountable for their commitments and performance. They establish mechanisms for tracking progress and addressing issues promptly.

Feedback Culture: Self-disciplined leaders create a culture of continuous improvement by encouraging regular feedback and reflection. They lead by example by seeking feedback themselves.

A self-disciplined approach to team leadership ensures that the team operates efficiently and cohesively. It minimizes confusion, reduces inefficiencies, and enhances the team's collective productivity.

Sustainability: Nurturing Growth and Continuity

Sustainability in the team context is about nurturing an environment where growth and continuity are valued, ensuring that the team remains adaptable and effective over time. Here's how sustainability is embodied in team leadership:

Long-Term Vision: Leaders with sustainability in mind have a long-term vision for the team's growth and success. They emphasize that the team's efforts are part of a larger journey.

Succession Planning: They invest in the development of team members, identifying potential future leaders and providing them with opportunities for growth.

Knowledge Sharing: Sustainable leaders promote knowledge sharing within the team. They encourage team members to learn from one another and document best practices.

Adaptability: They recognize the need for the team to adapt to changing circumstances and challenges. Sustainable leaders guide the team in embracing change and innovation.

Balancing Well-Being: Sustainability also involves a focus on the well-being of team members. Leaders ensure that the team's work is sustainable in terms of workload and stress.

Sustainability in team leadership ensures that the team's efforts are not short-lived but contribute to long-term success and growth. It cultivates a culture of adaptability, resilience, and continuous learning.

Case Study: Emily's Team Leadership

To illustrate TEM™ in team context, let's explore the leadership journey of Emily, a manager in a software development company. Emily is responsible for leading a diverse team of engineers, designers, and product managers.

Hard Work: Emily sets a high standard for dedication within her team. She leads by example, often putting in extra hours to meet project deadlines and resolve critical issues. Her commitment to hard work inspires her team members to invest their best efforts in their work. She acknowledges and celebrates their achievements, reinforcing a culture of dedication.

Mental Strength: In times of project setbacks or conflicts, Emily demonstrates mental strength by remaining calm and composed. She encourages her team to express their concerns openly and listens empathetically. Emily facilitates team discussions to find solutions and learn from challenges. Her approach helps the team build resilience and maintain a positive outlook.

Self-Discipline: Emily creates a structured environment for her team's success. She ensures that team goals are aligned with the company's mission, and each team member understands their role. Emily establishes regular communication channels, conducts weekly status meetings, and provides clear expectations. Her disciplined approach fosters an organized and accountable team.

Sustainability: Emily takes a long-term view of her team's growth and continuity. She identifies emerging leaders within the team and mentors them to take on leadership roles in the future. Emily encourages knowledge sharing by organizing internal workshops and encouraging team members to document best practices. She also places a strong emphasis on work-life balance, ensuring that her team's well-being is a priority.

Emily's leadership within the team context showcases the integration of TEM™ principles. Her dedication, mental strength, self-discipline, and focus on sustainability contribute to a high-performing and cohesive team.

Implementing TEM™ in Team Context

To apply TEM™ principles effectively in team leadership, consider the following steps:

Set the Example: Lead by example, demonstrating the hard work, dedication, and values you expect from your team.

Cultivate Resilience: Foster resilience and mental strength within the team by providing support during challenges and encouraging open communication.

Establish Structure: Create a structured environment that promotes efficient collaboration, with clear roles, responsibilities, and communication channels.

Promote Accountability: Hold team members accountable for their commitments and performance, and establish mechanisms for tracking progress.

Foster Growth: Encourage a culture of continuous learning and growth, identifying emerging leaders and providing mentorship opportunities.

Embrace Change: Recognize the need for adaptability in a constantly evolving environment, and guide the team in embracing change and innovation.

Balance Well-Being: Prioritize the well-being of team members by ensuring that workloads are sustainable and stress levels are managed.

By incorporating these principles into your team leadership approach, you can create an environment where hard work, mental strength, self-discipline, and sustainability thrive. Your leadership will not only drive team success but also contribute to the growth and well-being of individual team members. Team leadership within the TEM™ framework becomes a catalyst for achieving collective excellence and realizing the full potential of your team's capabilities.

Chapter 13

TEM™ in Organizational Leadership Context

Leadership in the organizational context represents the pinnacle of the leadership journey. It involves steering the entire ship, navigating through complex waters, and setting the course for the future. Within the expansive framework of The Expansive Methodology (TEM™), the four pillars of hard work, mental strength, self-discipline, and sustainability take on a transformative role in shaping organizational leadership.

In this chapter, we explore how these TEM™ principles converge within the organizational context to create a culture of excellence, drive strategic initiatives, and foster sustainable success. It is at this level of leadership that the true potential of TEM™ becomes most evident, as leaders orchestrate the harmonious interplay of these principles to propel their organizations to new heights.

The Critical Role of Organizational Leadership

Organizational leadership represents the summit of leadership responsibility, where decisions and actions have far-reaching consequences. Leaders at this level are entrusted with the stewardship of the entire organization, including its vision, mission, and long-term goals. Effective organizational leadership is characterized by the ability to inspire, align, and drive the collective efforts of all stakeholders, from employees to shareholders.

In the TEM™ framework, organizational leadership extends beyond individual leadership traits; it becomes a philosophy that permeates the organization's culture and DNA. Let's explore how the four pillars of hard work, mental strength, self-discipline, and sustainability manifest within this overarching context.

Hard Work: Cultivating a Culture of Excellence

Hard work in the organizational context goes beyond individual effort; it becomes the cornerstone of the organizational culture, fostering a commitment to excellence at every level. Here's how hard work is manifested in organizational leadership:

Visionary Leadership: Leaders who embody hard work set a visionary tone for the organization. They tirelessly pursue ambitious goals and inspire others to join them on the journey.

Dedication to Quality: A culture of hard work prioritizes quality in all aspects of the organization's operations. Teams are encouraged to go the extra mile to deliver exceptional products and services.

Continuous Innovation: Leaders drive a culture of innovation, challenging the status quo and encouraging teams to constantly seek improvements and new opportunities.

Recognition and Rewards: Hard work is recognized and rewarded throughout the organization. This recognition reinforces the commitment to excellence.

Collaborative Spirit: Teams work collaboratively, sharing ideas and expertise to achieve common goals. Hardworking leaders foster an environment where collaboration is valued and expected.

Adaptation to Change: In the face of change and challenges, hardworking leaders maintain resilience and adaptability. They guide the organization through transformations with determination and grace.

Hard work in organizational leadership sets the tone for a culture of excellence, where every individual is motivated to contribute their best efforts and where the pursuit of greatness is a collective endeavor.

Mental Strength: Navigating Complexity and Change

Mental strength in the organizational context equips leaders to navigate the complexities and uncertainties that come with steering a large ship. Here's how mental strength is expressed in organizational leadership:

Emotional Resilience: Leaders with mental strength maintain emotional resilience in times of crisis and uncertainty. They provide a source of stability and reassurance for the organization.

Strategic Thinking: Mental strength empowers leaders to think strategically, anticipating challenges and opportunities on the horizon. They make decisions that align with the organization's long-term vision.

Crisis Management: When faced with crises, leaders with mental strength remain composed and effective. They lead crisis management efforts with clarity and decisiveness.

Change Leadership: Mental strength is essential in leading organizational change initiatives. Leaders communicate the need for change, inspire buy-in, and guide the organization through transitions.

Empowering Others: Leaders with mental strength empower their teams to navigate complexity and change with confidence. They foster a culture where adaptability and continuous learning are celebrated.

Mental strength in organizational leadership ensures that the organization remains resilient, adaptable, and capable of weathering storms and seizing opportunities amid uncertainty.

Self-Discipline:
Orchestrating Organizational Alignment

Self-discipline in the organizational context involves orchestrating alignment among diverse stakeholders, ensuring that everyone is moving in the same direction toward a common purpose. Here's how self-discipline is practiced in organizational leadership:

Strategic Planning: Self-disciplined leaders prioritize strategic planning, setting clear organizational goals and objectives. They ensure that every decision and action aligns with the strategic vision.

Effective Governance: They establish governance structures and processes that promote transparency, accountability, and ethical conduct throughout the organization.

Communication Mastery: Self-disciplined leaders are masters of communication, conveying the organization's vision, values, and priorities with clarity and consistency.

Resource Allocation: They allocate resources judiciously, ensuring that investments and expenditures are aligned with strategic priorities.

Performance Management: Self-disciplined leaders implement performance management systems that track progress toward goals, provide feedback, and encourage continuous improvement.

Decision-Making Frameworks: They establish decision-making frameworks that consider the long-term impact and consequences of choices, guiding the organization toward sustainable success.

Self-discipline in organizational leadership creates an environment of alignment, where all stakeholders understand their roles and responsibilities, and where decisions and actions are purposeful and coherent.

Sustainability: Fostering Long-Term Success

Sustainability in the organizational context involves fostering an environment where long-term success is not just a possibility but a core principle. Here's how sustainability is embodied in organizational leadership:

Visionary Stewardship: Leaders with sustainability in mind act as visionary stewards of the organization, considering its long-term impact on society, the environment, and all stakeholders.

Talent Development: They invest in talent development, identifying and nurturing future leaders who will carry the organization forward.

Innovation Ecosystem: Sustainable leaders cultivate an innovation ecosystem, where new ideas and technologies are harnessed to adapt and thrive in changing landscapes.

Responsible Governance: They prioritize responsible governance, ensuring that the organization's operations are conducted ethically and in alignment with its values.

Community Engagement: Sustainability extends to community engagement, where leaders recognize their organization's role in making a positive difference in the broader community.

Balancing Profit and Purpose: Leaders strike a balance between profitability and purpose, recognizing that sustainable success encompasses financial stability and societal impact.

Sustainability in organizational leadership ensures that the organization not only survives but thrives over the long term, leaving a positive legacy for future generations.

Case Study:
Sarah's Organizational Leadership

To illustrate TEM™ in organizational context, let's examine the leadership journey of Sarah, the CEO of a global technology company. Sarah's leadership exemplifies the integration of TEM™ principles in steering an organization to excellence.

Hard Work: Sarah's leadership is marked by an unwavering commitment to hard work. She sets ambitious goals for the organization and inspires her team to achieve them. Sarah invests time in fostering a culture of dedication, where employees are motivated to go above and beyond to deliver exceptional results. Her dedication to quality and innovation permeates the organization's culture, resulting in cutting-edge products and services.

Mental Strength: In her role as CEO, Sarah demonstrates mental strength by navigating the complexities of the technology industry with foresight and strategic thinking. She remains calm and composed during crises, leading the organization through challenges with clarity and resolve. Sarah's ability to communicate a compelling vision and empower her teams to adapt to rapid technological changes has been instrumental in the company's success.

Self-Discipline: Sarah is a self-disciplined leader who prioritizes organizational alignment. She leads the strategic planning process meticulously, ensuring that every decision aligns with the company's long-term vision. Sarah has established effective governance structures that promote transparency, ethical conduct, and accountability. Her clear and consistent communication keeps all stakeholders informed and engaged in the pursuit of common goals.

Sustainability: Sarah's leadership embodies sustainability in its broadest sense. She views the organization as a steward of technology and innovation, ensuring that its impact on society and the environment is positive and enduring. Sarah invests in talent development, identifying emerging leaders and providing opportunities for growth. Her commitment to responsible governance and community engagement has earned the company a reputation for ethical leadership and societal contribution.

Sarah's organizational leadership showcases the profound impact of TEM™ principles. Her hard work, mental strength, self-discipline, and focus on sustainability have propelled the organization to a position of industry leadership and societal responsibility.

Implementing TEM™ in Organizational Context

To apply TEM™ principles effectively in organizational leadership, consider the following steps:

Set a Visionary Tone: As a leader, set a visionary tone for the organization, inspiring others to pursue ambitious goals and a commitment to excellence.

Foster Resilience: Cultivate resilience and adaptability within the organization, enabling it to navigate complexity and change effectively.

Establish Strategic Alignment: Orchestrate alignment among diverse stakeholders by prioritizing strategic planning, transparent governance, and effective communication.

Promote Sustainability: Foster an environment where long-term success is a core principle, considering the organization's impact on society, the environment, and all stakeholders.

Balance Profit and Purpose: Strike a balance between profitability and purpose, recognizing that sustainable success encompasses financial stability and societal impact.

By incorporating these principles into your organizational leadership approach, you can create an environment where hard work, mental strength, self-discipline, and sustainability converge to drive excellence, innovation, and lasting success. Organizational leadership within the TEM™ framework becomes a transformative force that shapes the organization's destiny and leaves a legacy of enduring impact.

Chapter 14

TEM™ in
Alliance Leadership Context

The concept of alliances holds a pivotal position. Alliances, whether they are partnerships between organizations or collaborations between individuals, require a unique set of leadership skills and principles to thrive. Within the expansive framework of The Expansive Methodology (TEM™), the four pillars of hard work, mental strength, self-discipline, and sustainability converge to shape leadership within the alliance context.

This chapter delves into the intricate dynamics of leadership within alliances, shedding light on how TEM™ principles can be harnessed to create harmonious and productive partnerships. It is within the alliance context that the importance of effective leadership becomes most pronounced, as leaders navigate the delicate balance between shared goals and individual interests.

The Strategic Significance of Alliance Leadership

Alliance leadership represents a distinct realm of leadership, characterized by the need to foster collaboration and synergy among entities with potentially divergent interests. Whether it's a business partnership, a research collaboration, or a coalition of like-minded individuals, effective alliance leadership is marked by the ability to align diverse stakeholders toward common objectives while respecting their autonomy.

In the TEM™ framework, alliance leadership stands as a testament to the adaptability and universality of its principles. Let's explore how the four pillars of hard work, mental strength, self-discipline, and sustainability manifest within this multifaceted context.

Hard Work: Cultivating Trust Through Commitment

In the alliance context, hard work transcends individual effort and takes on a collective dimension. It becomes the cornerstone for building trust and commitment among alliance members. Here's how hard work is realized in alliance leadership:

Shared Objectives: Leaders within alliances set clear and shared objectives that reflect the common goals of the partnership. These objectives become the focal point for collective effort.

Mutual Investment: Hardworking leaders emphasize the importance of mutual investment. Each alliance member is expected to contribute their fair share of resources, effort, and expertise.

Transparency: Leaders foster a culture of transparency within the alliance, ensuring that all members are informed about the progress, challenges, and successes of the partnership.

Conflict Resolution: When conflicts or disagreements arise, hardworking leaders address them promptly and constructively. They view conflicts as opportunities for growth and strengthening the alliance.

Celebrating Milestones: Recognizing and celebrating milestones and achievements within the alliance reinforces the culture of hard work and dedication.

Adaptation: Leaders emphasize the need for adaptability and resilience within the alliance. They encourage members to respond to changing circumstances with determination and flexibility.

Hard work within alliances establishes the foundation for trust and commitment. It sends a powerful message that each member is dedicated to the partnership's success and is willing to invest the necessary effort.

Mental Strength: Navigating Complexity and Diversity

Mental strength within the alliance context equips leaders to navigate the complexities of diverse perspectives, interests, and organizational cultures. Here's how mental strength is expressed in alliance leadership:

Emotional Intelligence: Leaders with mental strength possess high emotional intelligence, enabling them to empathize with the needs and concerns of alliance members.

Conflict Resolution: They facilitate open and constructive dialogue when conflicts arise. Mental strength allows leaders to mediate disputes and find common ground.

Cultural Sensitivity: Leaders understand and respect the cultural differences that may exist among alliance members. They promote a culture of inclusivity and mutual respect.

Strategic Alignment: Mental strength enables leaders to align the alliance's strategic direction with the evolving needs of all stakeholders.

Change Management: Leaders navigate changes and uncertainties within the alliance with resilience and adaptability. They communicate changes effectively and inspire confidence.

Empowering Collaboration: Mental strength empowers leaders to create an environment where collaboration is valued and where alliance members are encouraged to contribute their unique perspectives and expertise.

Mental strength in alliance leadership fosters an atmosphere of trust and collaboration, where members are confident that their voices are heard and their interests are considered.

Self-Discipline: Orchestrating Cooperation

Self-discipline within the alliance context involves orchestrating cooperation and ensuring that all members adhere to agreed-upon guidelines and commitments. Here's how self-discipline is practiced in alliance leadership:

Clear Governance: Leaders establish clear governance structures and processes that define roles, responsibilities, and decision-making mechanisms within the alliance.

Effective Communication: Self-disciplined leaders prioritize effective communication, ensuring that information flows seamlessly among alliance members.

Alignment with Objectives: They continually align alliance activities with the agreed-upon objectives, focusing on outcomes that benefit all stakeholders.

Accountability: Leaders hold alliance members accountable for their commitments and contributions. They establish mechanisms for monitoring progress and addressing deviations.

Ethical Conduct: Self-disciplined leaders emphasize ethical conduct within the alliance, promoting transparency, fairness, and integrity in all interactions.

Conflict Resolution: In the face of conflicts or disagreements, leaders maintain self-discipline by guiding the alliance toward solutions that serve its collective interests.

Self-discipline in alliance leadership creates a structured environment where collaboration and cooperation thrive, enabling members to work together effectively toward shared goals.

Sustainability: Ensuring Long-Term Viability

Sustainability in the alliance context involves ensuring the long-term viability and relevance of the partnership. Here's how sustainability is embodied in alliance leadership:

Strategic Foresight: Leaders with sustainability in mind consider the future viability of the alliance. They anticipate changing circumstances and plan accordingly.

Resource Allocation: Sustainable leaders allocate resources judiciously, ensuring that investments in the alliance yield long-term benefits.

Relationship Nurturing: They recognize the importance of nurturing relationships within the alliance, fostering trust and collaboration among members.

Adaptability: Sustainable leaders guide the alliance in adapting to evolving needs and challenges, ensuring that it remains a dynamic and relevant entity.

Knowledge Sharing: They promote knowledge sharing among alliance members, facilitating the exchange of expertise and best practices.

Continuous Improvement: Sustainable leaders encourage a culture of continuous improvement within the alliance, seeking opportunities to enhance its effectiveness and impact.

Sustainability in alliance leadership ensures that the partnership remains resilient, relevant, and capable of weathering challenges and changes over time.

Case Study: David's Alliance Leadership

To illustrate TEM™ in alliance context, let's delve into the leadership journey of David, a seasoned executive responsible for managing strategic alliances in a multinational corporation.

Hard Work: David's alliance leadership is characterized by a strong commitment to hard work. He understands that alliances require sustained effort to thrive. David actively engages with alliance partners, investing time and resources to build trust and collaboration. His dedication to achieving shared objectives is evident in his tireless efforts to ensure that alliance projects remain on track.

Mental Strength: In navigating the complexities of diverse alliances, David demonstrates mental strength. He possesses exceptional emotional intelligence, which allows him to understand the varying perspectives and cultural nuances of different partners. When conflicts arise, David remains composed and employs his mediation skills to foster constructive dialogue and find common ground. His adaptability and resilience enable him to lead alliances through dynamic changes in the business landscape.

Self-Discipline: David's self-discipline is evident in his meticulous approach to alliance management. He establishes clear governance structures for each alliance, defining roles, responsibilities, and decision-making processes. Effective communication is a priority, and he ensures that information flows seamlessly among alliance members. David holds partners accountable for their commitments and contributions, and he upholds the highest ethical standards within the alliances he manages.

Sustainability: David takes a long-term view of alliance viability. He continuously assesses the strategic relevance of each alliance, adapting alliance activities to align with changing market dynamics. Resource allocation is carefully managed to maximize the long-term impact of the partnerships. David fosters a culture of knowledge sharing among alliance members, and he encourages ongoing improvement and innovation within the alliances to ensure their sustainability.

David's alliance leadership embodies the integration of TEM™ principles. His hard work, mental strength, self-discipline, and focus on sustainability enable him to build and nurture successful alliances that drive growth and innovation for his organization.

Implementing TEM™ in Alliance Context

To apply TEM™ principles effectively in alliance leadership, consider the following steps:

Shared Objectives: Set clear and shared objectives that reflect the common goals of the alliance. Ensure that all members understand and commit to these objectives.

Cultural Sensitivity: Be sensitive to the cultural differences that may exist among alliance members. Promote a culture of inclusivity and mutual respect.

Effective Governance: Establish clear governance structures and processes that define roles, responsibilities, and decision-making mechanisms within the alliance.

Accountability: Hold alliance members accountable for their commitments and contributions. Implement mechanisms for monitoring progress and addressing deviations.

Sustainability Planning: Consider the long-term viability of the alliance. Anticipate changing circumstances and plan accordingly to ensure the alliance remains relevant.

Conflict Resolution: When conflicts or disagreements arise, facilitate open and constructive dialogue to find mutually beneficial solutions.

Resource Allocation: Allocate resources judiciously to maximize the long-term impact of the partnership.

Continuous Improvement: Foster a culture of continuous improvement within the alliance, seeking opportunities to enhance its effectiveness and impact.

By incorporating these principles into your alliance leadership approach, you can create an environment where hard work, mental strength, self-discipline, and sustainability converge to drive collaboration, trust, and the achievement of shared goals. Alliance leadership within the TEM™ framework becomes a catalyst for building lasting and productive partnerships that benefit all stakeholders involved.

The Expansive Method
A Blueprint
for Exceptional Leadership

As we conclude our exploration of The Expansive Methodology (TEM™) and its profound impact on leadership, we find ourselves standing at the threshold of a new era in leadership philosophy. TEM™ represents not just a set of principles but a comprehensive blueprint for exceptional leadership that transcends boundaries and adapts to a multitude of contexts.

Throughout this book, we've embarked on a journey to understand how the four pillars of hard work, mental strength, self-discipline, and sustainability converge to create leaders who inspire, unite, and guide others toward excellence. We've witnessed the transformative power of TEM™ in individual leadership, team dynamics, organizational stewardship, and alliance leadership. Now, let us reflect on the broader implications of this methodology and its potential to shape the future of leadership.

The Universality of TEM™ Principles

One of the remarkable aspects of TEM™ is its universality. It transcends industries, cultures, and generations, offering a timeless framework for leadership excellence. Whether you're a CEO leading a global corporation, a community organizer rallying volunteers, or an individual striving for personal growth, TEM™ principles remain relevant and adaptable.

Hard work, the cornerstone of TEM™, reminds us that dedication and effort are within our control, regardless of our circumstances or talents. Mental strength empowers us to navigate challenges with resilience and grace, fostering emotional intelligence and adaptability. Self-discipline instills order and purpose into our actions, guiding us to make deliberate choices aligned with our goals. Sustainability urges us to consider the long-term impact of our decisions on ourselves, our organizations, and society at large.

Leadership as a Dynamic Journey

TEM™ recognizes leadership as a dynamic journey rather than a static destination. Leaders who embrace this philosophy understand that growth and improvement are ongoing pursuits. They recognize that leadership is not confined to a title or position but is a mindset that can be practiced at every level of an organization and in every facet of life.

The TEM™ approach is characterized by continuous learning and adaptation. Leaders commit themselves to self-evaluation and feedback, recognizing that this process fuels their growth and enables them to better serve their teams and organizations. They understand that accountability is not a burden but a source of empowerment, driving them to take ownership of their leadership journey.

The Power of Team Leadership

TEM™ demonstrates its potency by creating high-performing, cohesive groups that achieve exceptional results. Leaders who embody TEM™ principles set the example for their teams, fostering cultures of hard work, collaboration, and innovation.

Evaluation becomes a tool for improvement, allowing teams to harness their collective strengths and address weaknesses constructively. TEM™ promotes open communication, ensuring that team members have a voice and are heard. In this environment, individuals thrive, and teams become more than the sum of their parts.

Team leadership within the TEM™ framework amplifies the impact of individual leaders, enabling organizations to adapt, innovate, and excel in dynamic environments.

Organizational Leadership as a Force for Change

At the organizational level, TEM™ principles shape the culture, strategy, and sustainability of enterprises. Visionary leaders who embody hard work inspire their organizations to reach new heights. They cultivate dedication to quality and innovation, establishing cultures of excellence that resonate throughout their organizations.

Mental strength equips leaders to navigate the complexities and uncertainties of the business world. They lead with emotional intelligence, making decisions that align with long-term vision and values. In times of crisis, they provide stability and guide their organizations through turbulent waters.

Self-discipline within the organizational context orchestrates alignment, ensuring that all stakeholders work together toward common objectives. Effective governance, communication, and accountability become the building blocks of an organization that operates with purpose and integrity.

Sustainability in organizational leadership ensures that enterprises not only succeed financially but also contribute positively to society and the environment. Leaders embrace their roles as stewards, fostering innovation, talent development, and responsible governance.

Organizational leadership within the TEM™ framework positions enterprises as drivers of positive change in the world.

Alliance Leadership as a Catalyst for Collaboration

In the alliance context, TEM™ principles facilitate collaboration and synergy among diverse entities. Leaders who apply TEM™ principles to alliances recognize the importance of hard work in building trust and commitment among partners. They understand that mental strength enables them to navigate the complexities of diverse perspectives and cultures.

Self-discipline becomes the glue that holds alliances together, fostering cooperation and adherence to agreements. Sustainable alliances thrive under leaders who plan for long-term viability, allocate resources judiciously, and promote knowledge sharing.

Alliance leadership within the TEM™ framework transforms partnerships into engines of innovation, growth, and shared success.

The Future of Leadership: A TEM™ Perspective

As we look to the future of leadership, it becomes evident that TEM™ offers a compass to navigate the ever-evolving landscape.

In a world where change is constant, and challenges are complex, TEM™ principles provide leaders with a foundation of unwavering values and adaptable strategies.

The leaders of tomorrow will be those who embrace the philosophy of hard work, dedicating themselves to continuous improvement and a tireless pursuit of excellence. They will harness mental strength to navigate the uncertainties of the digital age, fostering emotional intelligence and resilience in themselves and their teams.

Self-discipline will guide leaders in creating organizations and alliances that operate with transparency, accountability, and a commitment to ethical conduct. Sustainability will be at the forefront of their decision-making, as they consider the long-term impact of their actions on the world.

A Call to Action:
Embrace TEM™ Principles

As we conclude our journey through TEM™, we issue a call to action. Whether you are a seasoned executive, a budding entrepreneur, a community leader, or an individual striving for personal growth, embrace TEM™ principles as the cornerstone of your leadership philosophy.

Commit to hard work, recognizing that dedication and effort are the bedrock of achievement. Cultivate mental strength, equipping yourself to navigate the challenges and opportunities of an ever-changing world. Practice self-discipline, aligning your actions with your values and goals. Embrace sustainability, understanding that your decisions today have consequences that ripple into the future.

Remember that leadership is not a solitary pursuit but a journey of growth and collaboration. Involve others in your leadership journey, seek feedback, and hold yourself accountable. Create environments where hard work, mental strength, self-discipline, and sustainability are celebrated and practiced by all.

A New Era of Leadership

TEM™ ushers in a new era of leadership, one where values, adaptability, and a commitment to collective well-being take center stage. It is a philosophy that empowers leaders to transcend limitations, embrace challenges, and inspire others to reach their full potential.

In closing, remember that leadership is not defined by a title or position; it is defined by the impact you have on the world and the legacy you leave behind. As you embark on your own leadership journey, may TEM™ be your guiding light, illuminating the path to exceptional leadership and a brighter future for all.

Embrace TEM™. Lead expansively. Change the world.

Appendix A

TEM™ Implementation Resources

In the spirit of empowering readers to implement The Expansive Methodology (TEM™) effectively, this appendix provides a valuable collection of resources, worksheets, and tools. These practical aids are designed to facilitate your journey towards becoming an exceptional leader who embodies the core principles of hard work, mental strength, self-discipline, and sustainability.

Self-Assessment Worksheet: Begin your TEM™ journey by assessing your current leadership strengths and areas for improvement. This worksheet guides you through a structured self-assessment process, helping you gain insights into your leadership style and areas that may benefit from TEM™ principles.

Leadership Action Plan: Transform your insights into actionable steps with this leadership action plan template. Identify specific goals and strategies for incorporating TEM™ principles into your leadership approach. Use this tool to track progress and celebrate achievements along the way.

Team Alignment Checklist: For leaders focusing on team dynamics, this checklist aids in evaluating your team's alignment with TEM™ principles. Assess your team's commitment to hard work, mental strength, self-discipline, and sustainability, and identify areas where improvement is needed.

Organizational Sustainability Assessment: If you are an organizational leader, use this assessment tool to evaluate your organization's sustainability practices. Identify opportunities to enhance sustainability efforts, whether in environmental stewardship, social responsibility, or long-term viability.

Alliance Readiness Checklist: For leaders involved in alliances or partnerships, this checklist helps you assess your readiness to apply TEM™ principles to your collaborative endeavors. Ensure that your alliance aligns with the values of hard work, mental strength, self-discipline, and sustainability.

Communication and Feedback Guide: Effective communication is central to TEM™ leadership. Use this guide to enhance your communication skills, both as a speaker and a listener. Learn strategies for delivering clear, empathetic messages and fostering open dialogue within your leadership context.

Self-Assessment Worksheet: Begin your TEM™ journey by assessing your current leadership strengths and areas for improvement. This worksheet guides you through a structured self-assessment process, helping you gain insights into your leadership style and areas that may benefit from TEM™ principles.

Self-Assessment Worksheet: Evaluating Your Leadership in the TEM™ Framework

Self-assessment is a critical first step on your journey toward becoming an exceptional leader within The Expansive Methodology (TEM™) framework. This worksheet is designed to help you evaluate your current leadership strengths and areas that may benefit from the integration of TEM™ principles. As you work through this worksheet, reflect honestly on your leadership practices and consider how the four pillars of hard work, mental strength, self-discipline, and sustainability apply to your leadership style.

Section 1: Hard Work

Commitment to Excellence: On a scale of 1 to 10, rate your commitment to delivering excellence in your role. (1 = Minimal commitment, 10 = Full commitment)

Rating: _____

Effort Invested: Reflect on your recent projects or responsibilities. How much effort do you consistently invest to achieve the desired results? Describe specific examples.

Example: "I recently led a team project and put in extra hours to ensure we met the deadline."

Inspiring Dedication: Do you inspire dedication and hard work in your team or peers? How do you motivate others to give their maximum effort?

Example: "I encourage my team by setting high standards and recognizing their contributions."

Section 2: Mental Strength

Emotional Intelligence: Rate your level of emotional intelligence in your interactions with others. (1 = Low emotional intelligence, 10 = High emotional intelligence)

Rating: _____

Adaptability: Share an example of a recent situation where you demonstrated adaptability and resilience in the face of challenges or change.

Example: "During a sudden market shift, I led my team in reevaluating our strategy and successfully pivoted our approach."

Conflict Resolution: Describe a recent instance in which you effectively mediated a conflict or disagreement among team members or colleagues.

Example: "I facilitated a discussion between two team members with differing opinions, helping them find common ground."

Section 3: Self-Discipline

Alignment with Goals: How well do your actions align with your personal and professional goals? Rate your level of self-discipline in this regard. (1 = Poor alignment, 10 = Strong alignment)

Rating: _____

Transparency and Accountability: Share an example of a situation where you demonstrated transparency and accountability in your leadership role.

Example: "I openly acknowledged a mistake I made in a project and took responsibility for finding a solution."

Effective Governance: Do you have systems or processes in place to ensure that your team or organization operates with self-discipline? Describe them.

Example: "We have established weekly check-ins to review progress and ensure everyone is aligned with our objectives."

Section 4: Sustainability

Long-Term Impact: Reflect on your recent decisions and actions. How do they consider the long-term impact on your organization, community, or the environment?

Example: "I initiated a sustainability initiative in our company to reduce our carbon footprint and promote responsible practices."

Resource Allocation: Are you judicious in allocating resources to ensure long-term success? Describe how you prioritize resource allocation.

Example: "I allocate budget resources based on the potential for long-term growth and return on investment."

Ethical Leadership: Share an example of how you demonstrate ethical leadership by upholding principles of integrity and fairness.

Example: "I actively promote ethical conduct by fostering a culture of honesty and transparency in our organization."

Section 5: Reflection and Action

Reflect on your responses in each section and identify specific areas where you believe you can enhance your leadership by applying TEM™ principles. Consider the following:

Which TEM™ pillar do you believe is your strongest suit in leadership?

Which TEM™ pillar could benefit from more attention and development?

What actions can you take to further integrate TEM™ principles into your leadership style?

Are there specific goals or projects where you can immediately apply TEM™ principles to achieve better results?

Personal Action Plan:

Select one area from your self-assessment where you believe there is room for improvement.

Set specific, measurable, achievable, relevant, and time-bound (SMART) goals for enhancing this aspect of your leadership.

Example: "I will enhance my commitment to excellence by setting clear performance goals for my team and regularly reviewing progress. I will measure success by a 15% increase in project completion ahead of schedule over the next quarter."

Identify actions or strategies you will implement to achieve your SMART goals.

Example: "I will schedule weekly team meetings to discuss project status and identify any roadblocks. I will also provide additional resources or training to team members as needed to support their efforts."

Establish a timeline for achieving your goals and track your progress regularly.

Example: "I will begin implementing these changes immediately and will assess progress at the end of each month."

Share your goals and action plan with a trusted colleague, mentor, or coach who can provide guidance and accountability.

Remember that leadership development is an ongoing journey. By continuously assessing your leadership in the context of TEM™ principles and taking deliberate actions for improvement, you can progress toward becoming an exceptional leader who inspires positive change in your organization and beyond.

Leadership Action Plan: Transform your insights into actionable steps with this leadership action plan template. Identify specific goals and strategies for incorporating TEM™ principles into your leadership approach. Use this tool to track progress and celebrate achievements along the way.

Leadership Action Plan: Integrating TEM™ Principles for Exceptional Leadership

Creating a Leadership Action Plan is a vital step in your journey toward becoming an exceptional leader within The Expansive Methodology (TEM™) framework. This plan will guide you in translating insights from your self-assessment into actionable steps that align with TEM™ principles. Use the following template to set specific, measurable, achievable, relevant, and time-bound (SMART) goals and strategies for enhancing your leadership.

1. Leadership Pillar Focus

Select one or more TEM™ pillars that you would like to prioritize in your leadership development. (e.g., Hard Work, Mental Strength, Self-Discipline, Sustainability)

2. SMART Goals

Define specific, measurable, and time-bound goals related to the chosen TEM™ pillar(s). Ensure that your goals are realistic and aligned with your leadership aspirations.

Goal 1

Pillar Focus: (e.g., Hard Work)

SMART Goal: (e.g., Increase team productivity by 20% within the next quarter by fostering a culture of hard work and dedication.)

Measurement Metric: (e.g., Percentage increase in project completion ahead of schedule)

Timeline: (e.g., Within the next quarter)

Goal 2 (Optional)

Pillar Focus: (e.g., Mental Strength)

SMART Goal: (e.g., Enhance team resilience by providing training in stress management techniques, resulting in a 30% decrease in stress-related absenteeism over six months.)

Measurement Metric: (e.g., Percentage reduction in stress-related absenteeism)

Timeline: (e.g., Over six months)

3. Strategies and Actions

Outline the strategies and actions you will implement to achieve each SMART goal. Be specific about the steps you will take to integrate TEM™ principles into your leadership.

Strategies and Actions for Goal 1

Action 1: (e.g., Schedule weekly team meetings to discuss project status and roadblocks.)

Action 2: (e.g., Recognize and reward team members who consistently demonstrate hard work and dedication.)

Action 3: (e.g., Provide additional resources or training to team members as needed to support their efforts.)

Strategies and Actions for Goal 2 (Optional)

Action 1: (e.g., Collaborate with HR to organize stress management workshops.)

Action 2: (e.g., Encourage open communication and regular check-ins with team members to identify and address stressors.)

Action 3: (e.g., Share stress reduction techniques and resources with the team.)

4. Timeline

Establish a timeline for each action item, specifying when you will initiate and complete these actions.

Timeline for Goal 1

Action 1: Start immediately, complete within two weeks.

Action 2: Ongoing recognition and rewards.

Action 3: Initiate within one month, ongoing as needed.

Timeline for Goal 2 (Optional)

Action 1: Initiate stress management workshops within two months.

Action 2: Begin regular check-ins immediately, ongoing.

Action 3: Share stress reduction techniques and resources within one month.

5. Accountability

Identify individuals or stakeholders who will hold you accountable for achieving your SMART goals and executing your strategies. This could be a mentor, colleague, or a trusted advisor.

Accountability for Goal 1

Accountability Partner: (e.g., Your direct supervisor)

Check-in Frequency: (e.g., Monthly)

Accountability for Goal 2 (Optional)

Accountability Partner: (e.g., HR Manager)

Check-in Frequency: (e.g., Bi-monthly)

6. Progress Tracking:

Specify how you will track your progress toward each goal and action item. Regularly assess your achievements and make necessary adjustments to stay on course.

Progress Tracking for Goal 1

Measurement Metric: (e.g., Monthly review of project completion rates)

Progress Tracking Tool: (e.g., Spreadsheet or project management software)

Progress Tracking for Goal 2 (Optional)

Measurement Metric: (e.g., Quarterly analysis of absenteeism data)

Progress Tracking Tool: (e.g., HR records and employee feedback)

7. Review and Reflection

Schedule regular intervals for reviewing your Leadership Action Plan, reflecting on your progress, and making any revisions or refinements necessary to achieve your goals.

Review and Reflection Frequency

(e.g., Monthly review of progress)

(e.g., Quarterly reflection on the effectiveness of strategies)

8. Celebration of Achievements

Acknowledge and celebrate your successes and milestones as you progress toward your goals. Recognizing achievements can motivate and inspire continued growth.

Celebration of Achievements

(e.g., Quarterly team recognition for project milestones)

(e.g., Personal reward for achieving stress reduction goals)

Your Leadership Action Plan is a dynamic tool that will guide your journey toward becoming an exceptional leader within the TEM™ framework. By setting SMART goals, defining clear strategies and actions, establishing accountability, and regularly tracking your progress, you will not only enhance your leadership but also inspire positive change in your organization and beyond. Embrace TEM™ principles, lead expansively, and shape a brighter future for yourself and those you lead.

Team Alignment Checklist: For leaders focusing on team dynamics, this checklist aids in evaluating your team's alignment with TEM™ principles. Assess your team's commitment to hard work, mental strength, self-discipline, and sustainability, and identify areas where improvement is needed.

Team Alignment Checklist: Evaluating TEM™ Pillars in Team Dynamics

Effective leadership within The Expansive Methodology (TEM™) framework extends beyond individual growth—it also encompasses fostering a culture of hard work, mental strength, self-discipline, and sustainability within your team. This checklist is designed to help you assess your team's alignment with TEM™ principles and identify areas where improvement may be needed. Use this tool as a guide to evaluate and enhance your team's dynamics and performance.

Section 1: Hard Work

Clear Objectives and Goals:

Are team objectives and goals clearly defined and communicated to all members?

Is there a shared understanding of the importance of hard work and dedication in achieving these goals?

Commitment to Excellence:

Do team members demonstrate a commitment to delivering high-quality work and achieving exceptional results?

Is there a culture of celebrating hard work and dedication within the team?

Effort and Contribution:

Do team members consistently invest maximum effort to accomplish tasks and projects?

Are team members recognized and rewarded for their dedication and contributions?

Section 2: Mental Strength

Emotional Intelligence:

Is there an awareness of and respect for each team member's emotional well-being?

Are conflicts and disagreements handled with empathy and emotional intelligence?

Resilience and Adaptability:

Does the team demonstrate resilience in the face of challenges and setbacks?

Are there mechanisms in place to support team members in developing mental strength?

Open Communication:

Is there a culture of open and honest communication within the team?

Are team members encouraged to express their thoughts, concerns, and ideas freely?

Section 3: Self-Discipline

Alignment with Goals:

Do team members align their actions and decisions with the team's goals and objectives?

Is there a shared commitment to self-discipline in adhering to team processes and standards?

Accountability and Transparency:

Are team members held accountable for their commitments and contributions?

Is there transparency in decision-making and resource allocation within the team?

Effective Governance:

Are there clear governance structures and processes in place to define roles and responsibilities within the team?

Does the team operate with a sense of order and purpose?

Section 4: Sustainability

Long-Term Impact:

Does the team consider the long-term impact of its decisions and actions on the organization or project?

Are there initiatives or practices in place that promote sustainability within the team's work?

Resource Allocation:

Are resources allocated judiciously to maximize the long-term impact of the team's efforts?

Is there a focus on optimizing resource use and minimizing waste?

Ethical Conduct:

Does the team uphold ethical principles, such as integrity and fairness, in its interactions and decisions?

Are there mechanisms for addressing ethical concerns or dilemmas that may arise?

Section 5: Reflection and Action

Reflect on the checklist responses and identify specific areas where your team excels in aligning with TEM™ principles and areas where improvement is needed. Consider the following:

Which TEM™ pillar(s) does your team excel in?

Which TEM™ pillar(s) could benefit from more attention and development within your team?

What actions can you take as a leader to enhance your team's alignment with TEM™ principles?

Personal Action Plan:

Select one or more areas from the checklist where you believe your team can improve its alignment with TEM™ principles.

Set specific, measurable, achievable, relevant, and time-bound (SMART) goals for enhancing these aspects of your team's dynamics.

Example: "We will enhance communication and emotional intelligence within the team by implementing regular team-building activities and workshops. We will measure success by conducting a follow-up survey in three months to assess improvements in team dynamics."

Identify actions or strategies you will implement to achieve your SMART goals.

Example: "We will schedule monthly team-building activities, such as group problem-solving exercises, to enhance communication and teamwork. Additionally, we will organize quarterly workshops on emotional intelligence and conflict resolution."

Establish a timeline for achieving your goals and track progress regularly.

Example: "We will begin implementing these changes immediately, with the first team-building activity scheduled for next month. We will conduct a survey after three months to assess progress."

Share your goals and action plan with your team members and encourage their active participation in achieving these objectives.

Remember that fostering alignment with TEM™ principles within your team is an ongoing journey. By assessing your team's dynamics and implementing targeted strategies for improvement, you can create a cohesive and high-performing team that embodies the values of hard work, mental strength, self-discipline, and sustainability. Your leadership within the TEM™ framework will inspire positive change and elevate your team's success.

Organizational Sustainability Assessment: If you are an organizational leader, use this assessment tool to evaluate your organization's sustainability practices. Identify opportunities to enhance sustainability efforts, whether in environmental stewardship, social responsibility, or long-term viability.

Organizational Sustainability Assessment: Applying TEM™ Principles

Assessing and enhancing sustainability within your organization is a pivotal step in aligning with The Expansive Methodology (TEM™). Sustainability goes beyond environmental considerations; it encompasses the long-term viability, ethical conduct, and responsible resource management of your organization. This assessment tool will guide you in evaluating your organization's alignment with TEM™ principles related to sustainability and provide insights to foster positive change.

Section 1: Sustainability Vision and Strategy

Sustainability Mission Statement:

Does your organization have a clearly defined sustainability mission statement that reflects its commitment to long-term viability, ethical conduct, and responsible resource management?

Is this mission statement communicated and understood throughout the organization?

Strategic Goals and Objectives:

Are there sustainability-related strategic goals and objectives integrated into your organization's overall strategic plan?

Do these goals align with TEM™ principles, including hard work, mental strength, self-discipline, and sustainability?

Sustainability Leadership:

Is there dedicated leadership or a sustainability committee responsible for driving sustainability initiatives within the organization?

Are sustainability efforts championed by top management?

Section 2: Environmental Stewardship

Resource Efficiency:

Does your organization actively seek opportunities to reduce resource consumption, such as energy, water, and materials, in its operations?

Are there documented efforts to improve resource efficiency and reduce waste?

Green Practices:

Are environmentally friendly practices integrated into your organization's daily operations and decision-making processes?

Is there a commitment to adopting sustainable technologies and renewable energy sources where feasible?

Environmental Impact Assessment:

Has your organization conducted an assessment of its environmental impact, including carbon footprint and waste generation?

Are there initiatives in place to mitigate and offset this impact?

Section 3: Social Responsibility

Ethical Conduct:

Does your organization uphold ethical principles, such as integrity, fairness, and social responsibility, in its interactions and decision-making processes?

Are there mechanisms for addressing ethical concerns or dilemmas that may arise?

Employee Well-Being:

Does your organization prioritize the well-being, health, and safety of its employees?

Are initiatives in place to support mental health and work-life balance?

Community Engagement:

Does your organization actively engage with and contribute positively to the communities in which it operates?

Are there community outreach programs or partnerships in place?

Section 4: Long-Term Viability

Financial Sustainability:

Does your organization have a financial sustainability plan that ensures its long-term viability and stability?

Are resources allocated judiciously to maximize long-term growth and resilience?

Innovation and Adaptability:

Is your organization open to innovation and adaptation to address changing market conditions and emerging challenges?

Are strategies in place to remain competitive and relevant in the long term?

Stakeholder Engagement:

Does your organization actively engage with stakeholders, including employees, customers, investors, and regulatory bodies, to ensure alignment with long-term goals and expectations?

Is there a feedback mechanism for stakeholders to voice their concerns and expectations?

Section 5: Reflection and Action

Reflect on the assessment responses and identify areas where your organization excels in aligning with TEM™ principles related to sustainability. Additionally, identify areas where improvement is needed. Consider the following:

Which TEM™ sustainability principles does your organization excel in?

Which sustainability principles could benefit from more attention and development within your organization?

What actions can you take as a leader to enhance your organization's alignment with TEM™ sustainability principles?

Personal Action Plan:

Select one or more areas from the assessment where you believe your organization can improve its alignment with TEM™ sustainability principles.

Set specific, measurable, achievable, relevant, and time-bound (SMART) goals for enhancing these aspects of sustainability within your organization.

Example: "We will establish a Sustainability Task Force to develop and implement a comprehensive sustainability strategy aligned with TEM™ principles. We will measure success by achieving a 20% reduction in carbon emissions within the next two years."

Identify actions or strategies you will implement to achieve your SMART goals.

Example: "We will conduct a thorough audit of our environmental impact, identify areas for improvement, and develop a roadmap for reducing emissions. Additionally, we will engage employees in sustainability initiatives and provide training on sustainability best practices."

Establish a timeline for achieving your goals and track progress regularly.

Example: "We will establish the Sustainability Task Force within one month and initiate the environmental impact audit within two months. Progress will be reviewed quarterly."

Share your goals and action plan with key stakeholders within your organization, including top management, employees, and sustainability champions.

By actively assessing and enhancing sustainability within your organization, you not only align with TEM™ principles but also contribute to a more resilient, responsible, and ethically grounded organization. Your leadership within the TEM™ framework will inspire positive change and create a lasting impact on your organization's sustainability journey.

Alliance Readiness Checklist: For leaders involved in alliances or partnerships, this checklist helps you assess your readiness to apply TEM™ principles to your collaborative endeavors. Ensure that your alliance aligns with the values of hard work, mental strength, self-discipline, and sustainability.

Alliance Readiness Checklist: Applying TEM™ Principles for Successful Partnerships

Entering into alliances and partnerships is a strategic move that requires careful consideration and alignment with The Expansive Methodology (TEM™) principles. This checklist will guide you in assessing your organization's readiness for alliances and partnerships while ensuring alignment with TEM™ pillars such as hard work, mental strength, self-discipline, and sustainability. Use this tool to evaluate your preparedness and identify areas for improvement.

Section 1: Strategic Alignment

Strategic Objectives:

Are your organization's strategic objectives clearly defined and communicated?

Have you identified specific goals and outcomes that you aim to achieve through alliances or partnerships?

Alignment with TEM™ Principles:

Do the goals of potential alliances align with TEM™ principles, including hard work, mental strength, self-discipline, and sustainability?

Are you seeking alliances that share your commitment to ethical conduct and responsible resource management?

Leadership Support:

Is there visible leadership support for pursuing alliances and partnerships as part of your organization's growth strategy?

Do leaders actively champion the integration of TEM™ principles into alliance efforts?

Section 2: Resource Readiness

Resource Assessment:

Have you conducted an assessment of your organization's resources, including financial, human, and technological capabilities, to determine readiness for alliances?

Are there surplus resources available for allocation to alliance initiatives?

Resource Allocation Strategy:

Have you developed a resource allocation strategy that outlines how resources will be allocated to support alliance efforts?

Does this strategy prioritize sustainability and long-term resource availability?

Risk Management:

Have you identified potential risks associated with alliances, including financial, operational, and reputational risks?

Are risk mitigation plans in place to address identified risks?

Section 3: Organizational Alignment

Cultural Alignment:

Is there a cultural alignment between your organization and potential alliance partners, with a shared commitment to TEM™ principles?

Do both organizations value hard work, mental strength, self-discipline, and sustainability?

Communication and Collaboration:

Does your organization have effective communication and collaboration mechanisms in place to facilitate interaction with alliance partners?

Are team members equipped with the mental strength to navigate collaborative challenges and conflicts?

Governance Structure:

Have you established a governance structure that defines roles, responsibilities, and decision-making processes within the alliance?

Does this structure promote self-discipline and accountability among alliance members?

Section 4:
Risk Assessment and Mitigation

Risk Assessment Process:

Have you implemented a comprehensive risk assessment process to identify potential challenges and obstacles that may arise during alliances?

Is there a proactive approach to evaluating risks and developing mitigation strategies?

Mental Resilience:

Are team members prepared to exhibit mental strength in the face of alliance-related challenges and setbacks?

Is there a focus on building mental resilience and adaptability within your organization?

Contingency Plans:

Have you developed contingency plans to address potential disruptions or deviations from alliance goals?

Are these plans aligned with TEM™ principles of adaptability and sustainability?

Section 5: Evaluation and Reflection

Reflect on the assessment responses and identify areas where your organization excels in alliance readiness and alignment with TEM™ principles. Additionally, identify areas where improvement is needed. Consider the following:

Which TEM™ principles does your organization excel in regarding alliance readiness?

Which principles could benefit from more attention and development within your organization's alliance approach?

What actions can you take as a leader to enhance your organization's alliance readiness and alignment with TEM™ principles?

Personal Action Plan:

Select one or more areas from the assessment where you believe your organization can improve its alliance readiness and alignment with TEM™ principles.

Set specific, measurable, achievable, relevant, and time-bound (SMART) goals for enhancing these aspects of alliance readiness.

Example: "We will enhance our cultural alignment with alliance partners by fostering a culture of open communication and collaboration within our organization. We will measure success by conducting regular surveys to assess cultural alignment with alliance partners."

Identify actions or strategies you will implement to achieve your SMART goals.

Example: "We will schedule cross-functional meetings to enhance communication and collaboration across departments. Additionally, we will provide training on cultural awareness and adaptability."

Establish a timeline for achieving your goals and track progress regularly.

Example: "We will initiate cross-functional meetings within one month and conduct the first cultural alignment survey within three months. Progress will be reviewed quarterly."

Share your goals and action plan with key stakeholders within your organization to ensure alignment and commitment to alliance readiness efforts.

By actively assessing and enhancing your organization's readiness for alliances and partnerships while aligning with TEM™ principles, you will be better equipped to navigate complex collaborations and contribute to the long-term success of your organization. Your leadership within the TEM™ framework will inspire positive change and foster productive alliances that drive growth and innovation.

Communication and Feedback Guide: Effective communication is central to TEM™ leadership. Use this guide to enhance your communication skills, both as a speaker and a listener. Learn strategies for delivering clear, empathetic messages and fostering open dialogue within your leadership context.

Communication and Feedback Guide: Fostering TEM™ Principles in Leadership

Effective communication and feedback are essential components of leadership within The Expansive Methodology (TEM™) framework. This guide will help you understand the significance of communication and feedback in aligning with TEM™ principles such as hard work, mental strength, self-discipline, and sustainability. It provides strategies and best practices for fostering a culture of open communication, evaluation, and accountability within your organization.

Section 1: The Importance of Communication

Effective communication is the cornerstone of successful leadership. It sets the foundation for understanding, collaboration, and alignment with TEM™ principles.

Alignment with TEM™ Principles:

Communication aligns with hard work when leaders convey clear expectations and encourage dedication to shared goals.

It reflects mental strength when leaders communicate with empathy, resolve conflicts, and provide emotional support.

Self-discipline is exhibited when leaders consistently and transparently communicate expectations and hold themselves and others accountable.

Sustainability is promoted through ongoing communication that reinforces long-term vision and ethical conduct.

Section 2:
Strategies for Effective Communication

Implementing strategies for effective communication enhances your leadership and strengthens TEM™ principles.

Active Listening:

Listen actively to team members, acknowledging their ideas, concerns, and feedback.

Demonstrate mental strength by being present in conversations and showing empathy.

Clarity and Transparency:

Clearly convey goals, expectations, and decisions to promote self-discipline and accountability.

Transparency aligns with sustainability by fostering trust and ethical conduct.

Consistent Messaging:

Ensure consistency in your messages to reinforce TEM™ principles and prevent misunderstandings.

Feedback Channels:

Establish multiple feedback channels, including one-on-one meetings, team discussions, and anonymous platforms.

Encourage self-discipline by providing constructive feedback that supports growth.

Section 3: The Power of Evaluation

Evaluation is a TEM™ principle that drives improvement and accountability. Effective evaluation requires open communication.

Regular Assessment:

Implement regular performance assessments aligned with TEM™ principles.

Assess hard work, mental strength, self-discipline, and sustainability in individuals and teams.

Constructive Feedback:

Provide constructive feedback that identifies strengths and areas for improvement.

Demonstrate mental strength by offering support and solutions during challenging times.

Recognition and Reward:

Recognize and reward hard work, mental strength, self-discipline, and sustainable practices.

This aligns with accountability and encourages the continuation of positive behaviors.

Section 4: Accountability Through Feedback

Accountability is essential in TEM™ leadership. Feedback plays a pivotal role in holding individuals and teams accountable.

Setting Expectations:

Clearly communicate expectations and responsibilities to promote self-discipline.

Set sustainable goals that align with TEM™ principles.

Feedback Loops:

Create feedback loops where individuals and teams can track progress and adapt.

This promotes sustainability by ensuring alignment with long-term goals.

Follow-Up and Action:

Follow up on feedback and evaluation with action plans and accountability measures.

Show commitment to hard work and self-discipline by addressing issues promptly.

Section 5:
Stories of Leaders Who Embraced Communication and Feedback

Inspiration often comes from real-world examples. Here are stories of leaders who successfully applied TEM™ principles through communication and feedback:

Story 1: John, a team leader, implemented regular one-on-one meetings with his team members, fostering open communication. This led to improved mental strength as team members felt heard and supported.

Story 2: Sarah, a department head, introduced a transparent evaluation process that recognized hard work and self-discipline. Her team's sustainability efforts gained momentum as team members saw their contributions valued.

Story 3: Michael, a CEO, encouraged feedback from all levels of the organization. His commitment to accountability and transparency drove sustainable decision-making and ethical conduct.

Section 6: Analysis

Effective communication and feedback are vital for leadership within TEM™. They enable alignment with hard work, mental strength, self-discipline, and sustainability principles, fostering a culture of continuous improvement and accountability. By implementing the strategies and practices outlined in this guide, you can elevate your leadership and inspire positive change within your organization and beyond.

Appendix B

Recommended Further Reading and References

Leadership is an ever-evolving field, and continuous learning is essential for growth and development. This section offers a curated list of recommended further reading and references to deepen your understanding of TEM™ principles and expand your leadership knowledge:

"Leaders Eat Last" by Simon Sinek: Explore the importance of leadership grounded in selflessness and a commitment to serving others. Simon Sinek's book delves into the concept of leaders who prioritize the well-being of their teams.

"Emotional Intelligence" by Daniel Goleman: Dive into the realm of emotional intelligence and its pivotal role in leadership. Daniel Goleman's work sheds light on how emotional intelligence contributes to effective leadership.

"The Five Dysfunctions of a Team" by Patrick Lencioni: Discover common challenges that teams face and strategies for building cohesive and high-performing teams. Patrick Lencioni's book offers insights into addressing teamwork issues.

"Leadership and Self-Deception" by The Arbinger Institute: Explore the concept of self-deception and its impact on leadership. This book provides valuable perspectives on overcoming self-deception to become a more effective leader.

"The Lean Startup" by Eric Ries: Delve into the principles of entrepreneurship and innovation. Eric Ries introduces the concept of the lean startup methodology, which emphasizes agility and adaptability in leadership.

"Sustainable Leadership: Honeybee and Locust Approaches" by Gayle C. Avery and Harald Bergsteiner: Investigate the concept of sustainable leadership and its ecological metaphors. This book offers a unique perspective on leadership sustainability.

"Alliances: An Executive Guide to Designing Successful Strategic Partnerships" by Ard-Pieter de Man: If you are involved in alliances, this book provides practical guidance on designing and managing successful partnerships.

"Mindset: The New Psychology of Success" by Carol S. Dweck: Explore the power of mindset in leadership. Carol Dweck's work highlights the significance of having a growth mindset for personal and professional development.

"The Innovator's Dilemma" by Clayton M. Christensen: Delve into the challenges of innovation in business. Clayton Christensen's book discusses how disruptive innovations can transform industries and leadership strategies.

"Leadership in War" by Andrew Roberts: Explore leadership through historical perspectives. This book examines the leadership styles of notable military leaders and their relevance in today's context.

Bibliography

Covey, S. R. (1989). "The 7 Habits of Highly Effective People: Powerful Lessons in Personal Change." Free Press.

Goleman, D. (1995). "Emotional Intelligence: Why It Can Matter More Than IQ." Bantam Books.

Collins, J. C. (2001). "Good to Great: Why Some Companies Make the Leap... and Others Don't." HarperCollins.

Kotter, J. P. (1996). "Leading Change." Harvard Business Review Press.

Pink, D. H. (2011). "Drive: The Surprising Truth About What Motivates Us." Riverhead Books.

Dweck, C. S. (2006). "Mindset: The New Psychology of Success." Ballantine Books.

Charan, R., Drotter, S., & Noel, J. (2001). "The Leadership Pipeline: How to Build the Leadership-Powered Company." Jossey-Bass.

Maxwell, J. C. (2018). "Leadershift: The 11 Essential Changes Every Leader Must Embrace." HarperCollins Leadership.

Pink, D. H. (2006). "A Whole New Mind: Why Right-Brainers Will Rule the Future." Riverhead Books.

Gladwell, M. (2008). "Outliers: The Story of Success." Little, Brown and Company.

Drucker, P. F. (2008). "Management Challenges for the 21st Century." HarperCollins.

Collins, J. C., & Porras, J. I. (1994). "Built to Last: Successful Habits of Visionary Companies." Harper Business.

Sinek, S. (2009). "Start with Why: How Great Leaders Inspire Everyone to Take Action." Portfolio.

Greenleaf, R. K. (2002). "Servant Leadership: A Journey into the Nature of Legitimate Power and Greatness." Paulist Press.

Senge, P. M. (1990). "The Fifth Discipline: The Art & Practice of The Learning Organization." Doubleday.

Lencioni, P. (2002). "The Five Dysfunctions of a Team: A Leadership Fable." Jossey-Bass.

Adair, J. E. (2007). "Effective Leadership: How to Be a Successful Leader." Pan Macmillan.

Blanchard, K., & Johnson, S. (2015). "The New One Minute Manager." William Morrow.

Kotter, J. P. (2012). "Leading Change, With a New Preface by the Author." Harvard Business Review Press.

Marquet, L. D. (2012). "Turn the Ship Around!: A True Story of Turning Followers into Leaders." Portfolio.

Maxwell, J. C. (2007). "The 21 Irrefutable Laws of Leadership: Follow Them and People Will Follow You." Thomas Nelson.

Goldratt, E. M. (2014). "The Goal: A Process of Ongoing Improvement." North River Press.

Drucker, P. F. (2008). "The Effective Executive: The Definitive Guide to Getting the Right Things Done." HarperCollins.

Kim, W. C., & Mauborgne, R. (2005). "Blue Ocean Strategy: How to Create Uncontested Market Space and Make Competition Irrelevant." Harvard Business Review Press.

Index

A

Abraham Lincoln 30
Accountability 9, 15, 35-36, 59, 65-72, 76, 88, 96, 104, 107, 121, 123, 136, 143-144, 149, 167
activism 30, 46
Acute Mentality 26
Adaptability 13, 15, 23, 26, 28, 37, 42-43, 58, 61, 105, 121, 136, 148, 155
advocacy 30, 46
Alliance Leadership Context 117
Angela Merkel 30
authenticity 2, 6, 9, 10, 12, 16, 85, 96

B

Barack Obama 21
Bryan Stevenson 21

C

change management 52, 120
character 6-7, 14-15, 42, 74
collaboration 15, 50, 71, 94, 100, 102-104, 107, 111, 118, 120-122, 124, 127-129, 161-163, 165
commitment 2, 8-10, 14, 16, 18-24, 27, 30, 34, 35, 38-39, 42-48, 58, 64, 66, 69, 80, 86-87, 89, 98, 102-103, 106, 110-111, 114-115, 118-119, 122, 128-130, 132, 135, 138, 147, 149, 153-154, 159, 161, 163, 168-169, 172
Communication 9, 14, 23, 49, 50-52, 54-56, 62, 68, 70, 96, 104, 113, 120, 133, 148, 161, 165-166, 168
consistency 8, 34, 37, 39, 67, 76, 96, 99, 113, 166
core values 34-35, 37-38, 42, 45, 47, 76, 84, 88, 90-91, 96, 99
courage 8-9, 14, 16, 34-35, 37-39, 48, 66-67, 71, 96, 98-99, 121, 128, 137, 150, 155
criticism 20, 37, 52, 76, 95

D

decision-making 35-36, 45, 47, 52, 61, 69, 85, 113
discipline 8-10, 16, 20-21, 34-39, 42-44, 48, 62, 74, 76, 78-82,
84-86, 88, 94, 96, 98, 102, 104, 106-107, 110, 112-113,
115-116, 118, 120-124, 126, 128-129, 132-133, 135-137,
147, 149, 151, 154, 159, 161, 165, 166-169
diversity 30, 46

E

ecosystem 43, 113
effort 7, 16, 18-22, 24, 29, 38, 43, 74-75, 78, 87, 94-95, 102-103,
110, 118-119, 122, 126, 129, 135-136, 148
Emotional Intelligence 13, 61, 84, 87, 95, 119, 136, 148, 172, 174
empathy 15, 53-54, 84, 95, 98, 148, 165-166
empower 10, 13, 16, 91, 94, 112, 114
Empowerment 13, 24
endurance 29
ethical conduct 9, 24, 39, 47, 62, 98, 112, 115, 121, 129, 137, 153,
159, 166, 169
ethical leadership 34, 38, 66, 115, 137
Evaluation 9, 57-61, 127, 162, 167

F

feedback 23, 28, 36-37, 39, 50, 52, 55, 58-60, 63, 68, 70-71, 76,
80-81, 84, 86, 88-91, 9-99, 104, 113, 127, 129, 144, 156,
165-169
foward-thinking 43, 113
framework 2, 6-7, 15, 22, 24, 59, 64, 67, 74, 84-86, 90-91, 94, 100,
102, 107, 110, 116, 118, 124, 126-128, 135, 141, 145, 147,
151, 157, 163, 165

G

Gandhi 38, 69
goals 6, 12, 14, 18, 20-23, 26-28, 31, 36-38, 42, 44, 47, 51-52, 54,
59-60, 62-63, 67-68, 71, 75-81, 85, 87-91, 102-104, 106,
110-115, 118, 121, 123-124, 126, 129, 132, 136, 138, 141,
143-145, 147, 149-151, 153-154, 156-157, 159, 162-163,
165-166, 168

Growth Mindset 19, 27-28, 70

H

Hard Work 7, 16-18, 21-22, 43, 74-75, 79-80, 86, 90, 94, 98, 102, 106, 110, 114, 118, 122, 135, 141, 147

I

improvement 7-9, 16, 18-19, 22-24, 37, 43-44, 55, 5-61, 63-64, 76, 78-81, 84, 86-91, 95, 99, 103-104, 113, 122-124, 126-127, 129, 132, 135, 138-139, 147, 150-151, 156-157, 159, 162, 167, 169
inclusion 30, 46
Inclusivity 13
Indra Nooyi 38, 69
influence 6, 10, 12, 14, 50-51, 54, 56, 94
integrity 8, 9, 14, 16, 34-35, 37-39, 48, 66-67, 71, 96, 98-99, 121, 128, 137, 150, 155

J

John Lewis: 69

K

key performance indicators 58, 68

L

Leadership 2, 3, 6, 11-14, 28-29, 41-48, 50-51, 58-59, 65-67, 77-79, 81, 83-84, 86, 89, 93-94, 97, 101-102, 105, 109-110, 112, 114, 117-118, 122, 125-128, 130, 132, 135, 137, 141, 144-145, 154, 160, 165, 172-175
leadership brand 6-10, 12-16, 18, 22, 24, 34, 58

M

Malala Yousafzai 22
Malcolm X 30
Mary Barra 38, 69
mastery 19-20, 84-85, 90-91
Mental Strength 8, 16, 25-26, 30-32, 43, 74-75, 80, 87, 90, 95, 98, 103, 106, 111, 114, 119, 122, 136, 141-142, 148

N

Napoleon Bonaparte 38, 69
Nelson Mandela 7, 13, 30
non-verbal 51

O

One-to-One Leadership Context 93
Oprah Winfrey 21
Organizational Leadership Context 109

P

performance 8-9, 20, 37, 58-61, 68, 71, 98, 104, 107, 113, 138,
    147, 167
Perseverance Mindset 20
pillars 9-10, 15-16, 43, 66, 74-75, 77, 79, 81, 84-86, 94, 97, 102,
    110, 118, 126, 135, 141, 159
principles 3, 6, 7, 9-10, 12-14, 20, 34-39, 42, 44, 45, 47-48, 54-55,
    61-62, 67-68, 71, 76, 84-85, 88, 90-91, 96, 99, 102, 107,
    113-114, 127, 129-130, 133, 151, 159
purpose 2, 7, 9-10, 12, 14, 16, 44, 50-52, 71, 79, 85-86, 102, 112,
    114, 116, 126, 128, 149
Purpose-Driven 14, 86

R

resilience 7-8, 13, 15, 23, 26-27, 30-32, 43, 47-48, 58, 71, 76, 79,
    85, 87-88, 91, 98, 103, 105-107, 111, 115, 119-120, 122,
    126, 129, 136, 142, 148, 155, 162

S

self-awareness 9, 31, 37-38, 61, 63-64, 68, 84, 89-91
Self-Discipline 8, 16, 33, 34, 37-39, 44, 74, 76, 80, 88, 90, 96, 98,
    104, 106, 112, 115, 120, 122, 136, 141, 148
Self Leadership Context 83
self-reflection 1, 3, 39, 61-64, 66, 87, 90
Sheryl Sandberg 31
Shonda Rhimes 22
strategy 45, 153, 160, 175
stress management 27, 29, 85, 91, 142-143

Sustainability 8, 16, 41-45, 47, 48, 62, 74, 77-81, 88-90, 97-98,
        105-106, 113-116, 121-123, 126, 128-129, 133, 137, 141,
        149, 153-155, 157, 166
system 43, 113

T

Team Leadership Context 101
The Expansive Methodology 6-7, 10, 15, 60, 74, 84, 94, 102, 110,
        118, 126, 132, 135, 141, 147, 153, 159, 165
time management 23, 35, 39, 76
transparency 3, 6-7, 9, 10, 12-14, 20, 34-39, 42, 44, 45, 47-48, 54,
        55, 61-62, 67-68, 71, 76, 84-85, 88, 90-91, 96, 99, 102, 107,
        113-114, 127, 129-130, 133, 151, 159

V

values 3, 6-7, 9-10, 12-14, 20, 34-39, 42, 4445, 4748, 54-55, 61-
        62, 67-68, 71, 76, 84-85, 88, 90-91, 96, 99, 102, 107, 113-
        114, 127, 129-130, 133, 151, 159
vision 9-10, 14-15, 21, 22, 27, 38, 44, 47-48, 50-51, 77-78, 80-81,
        85-86, 88, 90-91, 102, 104-105, 110, 112-115, 127, 166

W

Warren Buffett 37, 69
Work Ethic Paradox 18

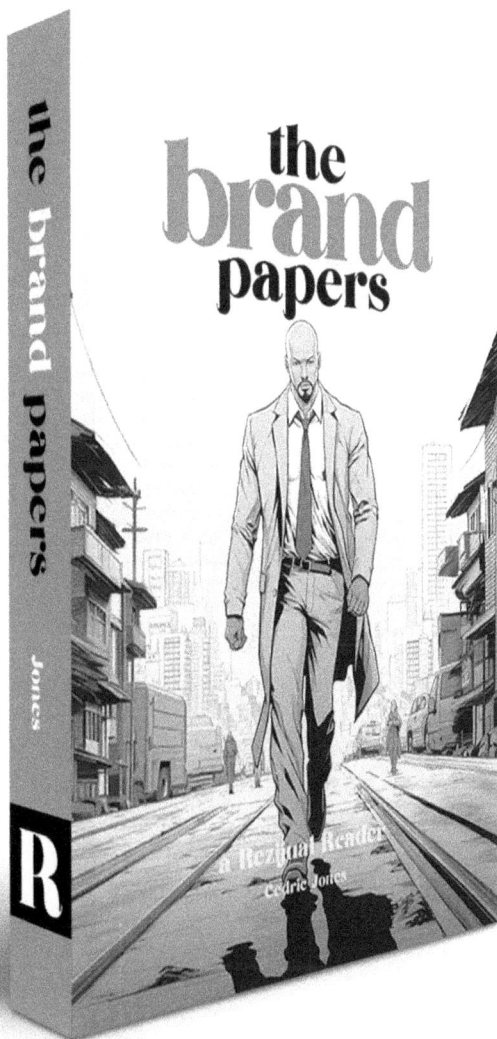